CREATIVE BONE

cool Crafts to Make

CAROL FIELD DAHLSTROM

even if you don't have a

creative bone

in your body!

or even if you do!

Carol Field Dahlstrom
Brave Ink Press
Ankeny, Iowa

Author and Editor
Carol Field Dahlstrom

Book Design
Lyne Neymeyer

Photography
Pete Krumhardt, Dean Tanner— Primary Image,
Andy Lyons Cameraworks, Lyne Neymeyer
How-to Illustrations: Kristen Krumhardt

Copy Editing: Jill Philby
Proofreading: Jan Temeyer, Elizabeth Dahlstrom
Props and Location: Roger Dahlstrom
Technical Assistant: Judy Bailey
Special thanks to these people for helping to make some
of the projects in the book: Susan Banker, Ardith Field, Barbara Hoover,
Margaret Sindelar, Ann E. Smith, Jan Temeyer

ISBN 0-9679764-6-4
Library of Congress Control Number: 2005900455

Separations: Scan Graphics, Des, Moines, Iowa
Printed in the United States of America
First Edition

While all of the information has been checked and tested, human error can occur.
Carol Field Dahlstrom Inc. and Brave Ink Press cannot be held responsible for any loss or injury
associated with the making of any project or information in this book.

Carol Field Dahlstrom, Inc. and Brave Ink Press strive to provide high quality products and
information that will make your life happier and more beautiful. Please write or
e-mail us with your comments, questions, and suggestions or to inquire about purchasing
books at braveink@aol.com or Brave Ink Press, P.O. Box 663, Ankeny, Iowa 50021.

Visit us at www.braveink.com to see upcoming books from Brave Ink Press
or to purchase books.

The "I can do that" books

Your Creative Style

Go ahead—admit it! You love to make things. Well, at least you love to think about it and admire those who do. It's time to find your creative style and flaunt it. Okay, maybe you say you don't have a creative bone in your body. Sometimes we all feel a little intimidated by certain things that we would like to make or do but we just haven't been shown the right way to do it. That is all about to change.

In this book we've taken the mystery out of being creative and making cool things. We show you every step of the way using easy-to-follow directions and down-to-earth illustrations. Plus we inspire you with all kinds of ways to use the wonderful things you make. We'll show you how to decorate with them, give them as gifts, and just enjoy them yourself.

So grab some scissors, roll out the paper, unfold the fabric, and dig out that yarn—it's time to show your creative side. There is no doubt that soon you'll be saying, "I can do that!"

Carol Field Dahlstrom

find it! Create it! Enjoy it!

Pick a project and have fun creating your work of art.
Pretty soon you'll be saying, **"I can do that!"**

how to use this book

Look how easy it is to be creative! First, you'll see the project that you will make. We'll give you a simple list of materials that you need and then give you some special tips that we learned as we made these cool projects ourselves. Next you'll find easy-to-understand illustrations that we created to make it simple to make the project. If you

Here is the list of supplies you need— they are all easy to find. We even tell you where you can find them.

Look at what you learn to make! You'll be inspired by the close-up photos of each project.

We give you special tips and secrets we have learned along the way.

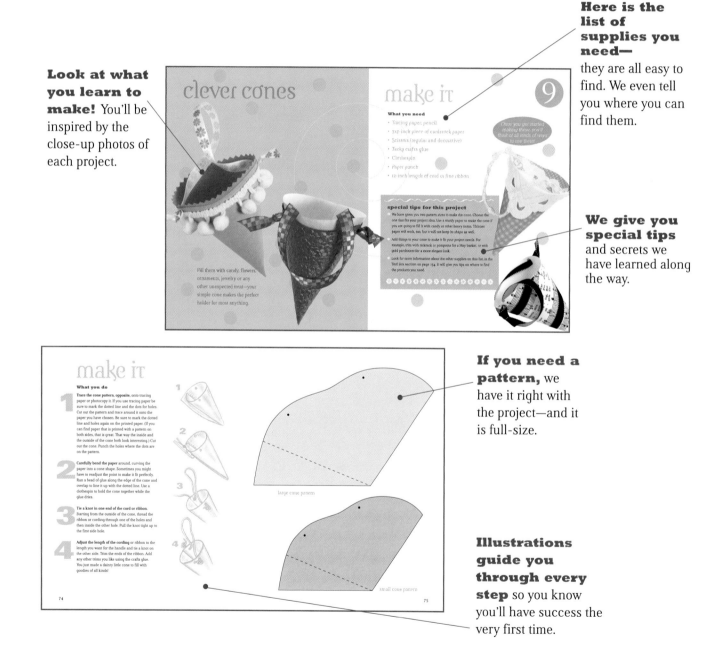

If you need a pattern, we have it right with the project—and it is full-size.

Illustrations guide you through every step so you know you'll have success the very first time.

need a pattern, it's right there, too—and full size. Then you'll be inspired by all the possibilities of what you can do to make this project fit your personal style. And finally, we'll show you all kinds of ways to use the project that you created. What could be easier? So go ahead and get started—its time to show your creative side!

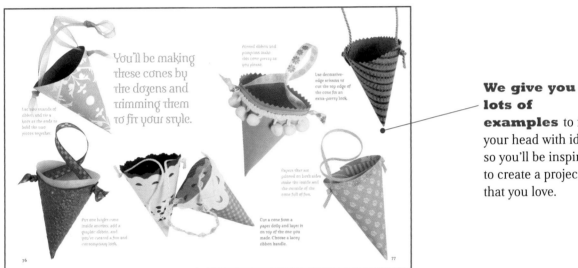

We give you lots of examples to fill your head with ideas so you'll be inspired to create a project that you love.

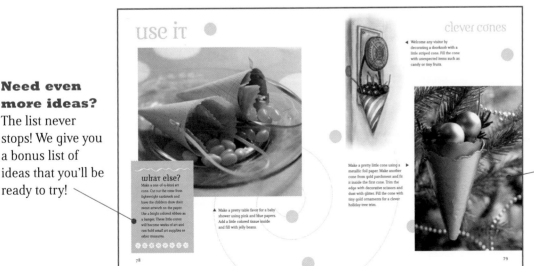

Need even more ideas? The list never stops! We give you a bonus list of ideas that you'll be ready to try!

We show you how to use it. After you learn to make your project, you'll find all kinds of uses for it. We give you lots of ideas in our beautiful photos.

fancy felt purses

Simple stitches and pretty colors of felt and ribbon combine to make these little bags totally cool.

make it

What you need

- Small rectangular piece of wool felt or acrylic felt
- Pencil; ruler; scissors
- Ribbon or cording for handle; straight pins
- Embroidery floss; needle; button

What you do

1 **First, plan the design of your purse.**
Use one of the diagrams on page 10 as a guide to cut the felt to make your purse, or make it the size you wish, designing the size to fit how you plan to use it. Cut the rectangle and then measure and mark it into three equal thirds. Lightly draw the two lines on the felt with a pencil.

2 **Cut the top third of the rectangle in whatever shape you wish for the flap.**
Fold the bottom third up to make the bottom of the purse and the top third (that you made into the flap) down to form the purse shape. Lay the button on the flap and make a light mark on both sides of it. Draw a line between the dots. Carefully cut a slit along the lines for the button hole. (You will do the buttonhole stitch around the edges of the hole later).

3 **Cut the ribbon or cording the length you like.** Lay the ribbon or cording at the edges of the purse between the layers. Pin in place with the straight pins.

special tips for this project

- Felt comes in acrylic or wool. Either will work, but the wool is a bit nicer to work with and can be washed or "felted" before you make the bag creating a textured look. See the Tool Box on page 154 for tips.

- You can use embroidery floss, perle cotton, or other fiber to work your running and buttonhole stitches. Check out the Tool Box section on page 154 to learn more about these types of fibers.

make it

Now you are ready to sew the purse together.
If you have never done any stitches of any kind
before, practice the running stitch and the
buttonhole stitch on a practice piece of felt. They
are really easy to do. You can hold your purse
together at the sides using either stitch.
The buttonhole stitch works best around the slit
for the buttonhole. You can decorate around the
flap with either stitch.

Thread the needle with at least 2 strands of the
embroidery floss. (Embroidery floss comes with
6 strands together. Carefully pull it apart to get the
two strands.) If you are using perle cotton, one
strand is fine. Start with a length of floss about
24 inches long. Tie a knot in the end of your floss
or thread. You can double the thread(s) and knot
them together or use just the single set of threads
and leave the short thread loose.

For the running stitch: The running stitch is very
easy to do. Use it to hold the purse together at the
sides and to decorate the flap if you wish.

4 **Step 4 A** Start with the knot on the back side. Pull
the needle up through the fabric, and then back
down again keeping the stitches about $1/4$-inch
long and about $1/4$-inch apart. When you are done
working the running stitch, secure the end by
taking 3 or 4 tiny stitches over each other in the
same place. Trim the threads.

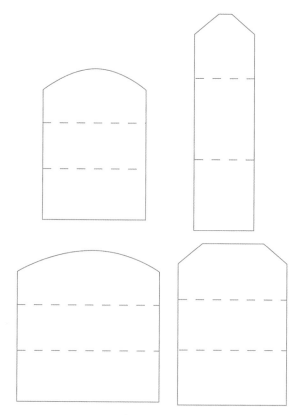

purse shape diagrams

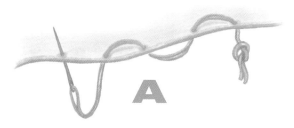

For the buttonhole stitch: The buttonhole stitch was designed to use around buttonholes to keep them stronger because a buttonhole gets a lot of use with the button going in and out. (So this one is a good one to use on the buttonhole on your purse!) You can also use it to hold the sides of your purse together or as a decorative stitch.

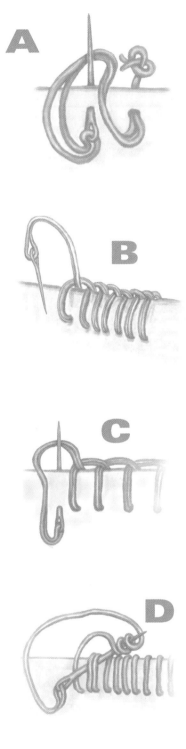

5

Step 5 A Starting with the knot on the back, and about $\frac{1}{4}$ inch from the edge of the fabric, pull the thread through the fabric. Make a loop with the thread and put the needle into the fabric about $\frac{1}{4}$ inch from the other hole then back up so the needle point is in front of the loop. Pull the needle up.

Step 5 B Bring the needle over the top and down, lining up where the needle goes in with the other holes you have made.

Step 5 C Continue to bring the needle back up straight, looping the thread behind it. Continue making the stitches until finished.

Step 5 D To finish, bring the needle up through the last stitch on the back side of the project or the underside of the flap, and wind the thread around the needle. Pull the needle through, making a knot. Cut off the remaining thread.

Sew the button in place so the buttonhole fits over it. You just made a cool felt bag!

This bag is made using "felted" fabric. Simply wash the wool felt in hot water before you make the bag and let it shrink up in the dryer to give it a wrinkled texture and softer feel.

A vintage button in white and silver makes this cute and tiny bag look even sweeter.

This clever little purse uses only the running stitch at the sides and flap. The handle is a lacey piece of trim.

You can design a felt (or felted) bag to hold just about anything you wish.

The bright colors of this little bag make it appealing to a teenager—maybe to carry some cool colors of lipstick or lip gloss.

This felted bag was designed to hold sunglasses or reading glasses.

A flat piece of ribbon serves as a handle for this little purse.

use it

what else?

Make a felt bag that just fits inside your bigger purse to carry coupons for grocery shopping. Try making a long thin felt bag to hold a favorite pair of scissors. Make tiny bags to hold money and hang them on the Christmas tree for a great gift idea or use the little bags to hold a secret message to give to a friend.

▲ Metallic threads are used to stitch up this little bag—making it sturdy (and cool enough) to hold a favorite take-along.

felt purses

Make a tiny bag and fill it with silk or dried flowers—then hang it on the wall for a pretty little decoration.

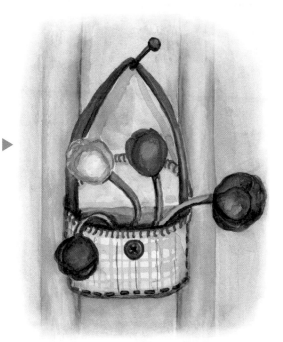

For the holidays, make a tiny red bag, trim it in gold, and use it as a gift holder for a piece of special jewelry.

A bright green felt bag is trimmed with matching floss and given a fun fiber handle to hold sweet treats.

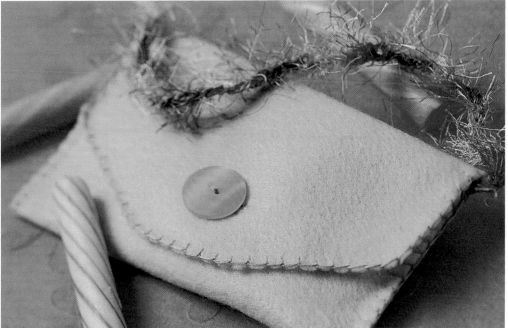

simple strands of beads

Beading is as easy as stringing beautiful pieces of glass or plastic onto a wire or cord. With just a few basic tips, you'll be making beaded fashions like a pro!

make it

②

What you need

(to make a beaded strand using wire and clasps)

• Beading wire (we like the .018" 26# 12 kg)

• Old scissors or wire snips; needle-nose pliers

• Necklace clasps; crimp beads

• Assortment of beads that you like

• Small square of felt to arrange your beads on

(to make a beaded strand on elastic cording)

• Elastic bead cording (we like the clear 1.00 mm .039")

• Assortment of beads that you like

• Small square of felt to arrange your beads on

• Scissors; masking tape

• Clear fingernail polish

These necklaces are so beautiful—don't tell anyone they were so easy!

special tips for this project

❋ Beading can sound complicated but beading is really very easy. The only two things you really need to know are how to choose pretty beads and how to secure the end of the beaded strand. You can finish your strand in one of two ways. If you use wire, attach a necklace or bracelet clasp. If you use cording, tie the end in a knot and secure with fingernail polish.

❋ For more information about the supplies you see in the supply list, check out the Tool Box on page 154.

17

make it

What you do

Prepare to make the strand. You can make a strand of beads for a necklace, a bracelet, a napkin ring, or many other uses. No matter what you want to make, choose beads that you like and arrange them on the piece of felt. The felt will keep the beads from rolling around so you can decide the order of your beads. Use spacer beads to add a professional touch. You can buy beads at crafts stores, discount stores, and bead stores. They range in price from very inexpensive to very expensive.

A. Lobster clasp B. Toggle clasp
C. Barrel clasp

To make a beaded strand using elastic cording: (This works best for bracelets, napkin holders, votive decorations or any time you need the strand to stretch.) Cut the elastic cording to the length you need plus 6 inches. Place a piece of masking tape over one end of the cording to keep the beads from falling off. String the beads in the order that you planned. Measure the strand to be sure it is the length you want. Adjust it if you need to.

Crimp beads

1 **Remove the tape and tie a square knot** with the elastic cording. Now tie another square knot to be sure it is secure.

2 **Place a drop of clear fingernail polish** on the knots. Allow to dry. Add another drop after the first one dries. (Wow, that was easy!)

To make a beaded strand on a wire with clasps:
(This works best for necklaces and fancy bracelets).
There are many kinds of clasps such as barrel,
lobster, and toggle. (See photo, opposite.)
Choose the clasp you like. Cut the wire the length
you want your strand to be plus 6 inches.

1 **In this illustration we are showing a barrel clasp.**
Thread one end of the wire through a crimp bead,
then through one end of the clasp and then back
through the crimp bead leaving about $1/2$ inch of
the wire tail.

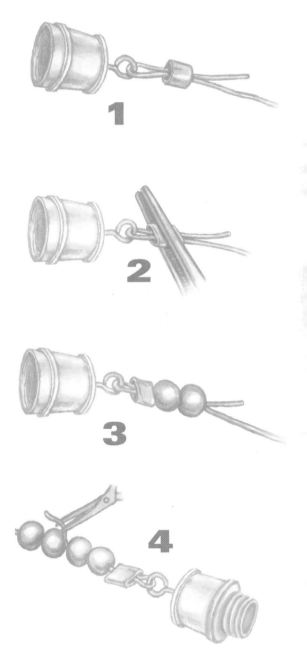

2 **Using the needle-nose pliers**, squeeze the crimp
bead to keep the wire from slipping out.
What you are really doing is smashing this tiny
bead—it looks so little, but it does work!

3 **Start stringing the beads** you have laid out on the
piece of felt in the order that you decided. Thread
over both wires up to the crimp bead and continue
to string the beads until you reach the length you
like. Common necklace lengths are 13, 16, and 18
inches. Common bracelet lengths are 7, 8, or 9
inches. (But you can make your jewelry any
length you wish because you are the artist!) End
with a crimp bead. Leave at least 4 inches of wire
remaining to attach the other end of the clasp.

4 **Loop the end of the wire** through the other end of
the clasp and back through the crimp bead.
Squeeze it with the needle-nose pliers as you did
at the beginning of your strand. Feed the wire tail
through at least two of the beads and cut off the
excess with old scissors or wire snips. Hold up
your pretty bead strand and watch it sparkle!

Choose a variety of beads that match your style. It's okay to use round and square beads together— you make the rules.

The focal point of this green-tone necklace is a set of long beads that come in gradual lengths.

Try using colors that have the same intensity. We chose a bright orange and a bright yellow-green. Set off the center bead with spacers.

Long silver beads make this necklace elegant as well as fun. Set plain blue round beads off with tiny seed beads on each side.

Try all kinds of beads in all kinds of combinations to create your own beading style.

One special bead is all it takes to make this elastic cord bracelet as cute as can be.

Large flat round beads combine with wire spiral beads for this fun-to-wear contemporary necklace.

use it

▲ String beads to match a pretty table setting and use as a napkin ring. The strand can be used as a bracelet for the lucky guest after the dinner party.

beaded strand

Make a votive candle holder even more special by surrounding it with its own set of bracelets. Use elastic cording to create a trio of beaded strands in colors that accent your candle.

Use silver charms and silver and red beads to make a bracelet that resembles the charm bracelets of years ago.

Make primary colors the theme for your selection of beads. Mix square and round beads for a fun and unexpected touch. ▼

what else?

Use beaded strands to trim a valance. Make the strands and secure both ends with small jump rings. Make as many strands as you need to make a beaded fringe. Tack one end of each of the strands in a row at the bottom of a purchased valance for a sparkling look.

pretty pinwheels

Pinwheels aren't just for kids!
Learn to make a simple
pinwheel and then let your
imagination spin all kinds of
ideas on how to use and display
this ageless craft.

make it

3

What you need

- 8-inch-long balsa wood stick or dowel
- Acrylic paint; small paintbrush
- 1 yard of ¼-inch-wide ribbon; white tacky glue
- 2 pieces of 7x7-inch printed medium weight paper glued back to back or one piece of cardstock printed on both sides
- Regular and decorative-edge scissors
- One ball-headed long straight pin
- 1-inch square of plastic fun foam
- One large bead (pony bead)
- Rubber eraser cut off from a new pencil

Don't let this long supply list fool you— these are a breeze to make!

special tips for this project

* You can find cardstock printed on both sides at crafts and discount stores. You can also use a lighter weight paper and glue two pieces together. For more information about papers and where to find them, look for the Tool Box section on page 154.

* We chose balsa wood sticks because they are lighter and pins go through balsa wood easier than a harder wood. A regular dowel will work, too.

* Look for more information about the other supplies on this list in the Tool Box section on page 154. It will tell you where you can buy them and about how much they cost.

make it

What you do

Prepare the pinwheel stick: Before you start making the paper pinwheel, paint the balsa stick with acrylic paint and set it aside to dry. After it is dry, dab a little white tacky glue on the back of the ribbon. Wind the ribbon around the stick. Add more glue if you need to. Set the stick aside to dry while you make the paper pinwheel.

Prepare the paper: If you need to glue the back sides of two pieces of paper together, use spray adhesive or a glue stick. (See the Tool Box, page 154, for more information about these adhesives.) If you are using a paper that is printed on both sides, you are set to go!

1 **Make the paper pinwheel:** Lay your paper square on a smooth table. Referring to the big pattern, opposite, use a ruler and pencil to lightly mark the dotted lines to the center circle. (Draw around a penny to make the center circle.) Carefully cut along the pencil lines just up to the middle circle. Don't cut too far. Mark the dots in the corners as they look on the pattern and mark a dot in the center.

2 **Starting with any dotted corner,** bend the paper to the center. Do this with every dotted corner.

3 **Place the long pin** through the plastic fun foam, through the top corner hole, and then through all of the corner holes and through to the back.

4 **Turn the pinwheel to the back.** Put the pony bead on the sharp end of the pin, then put the pin through the dowel and finally into the pencil eraser. Adjust the pinwheel as necessary so it spins. Smile at how cool your pinwheel looks.

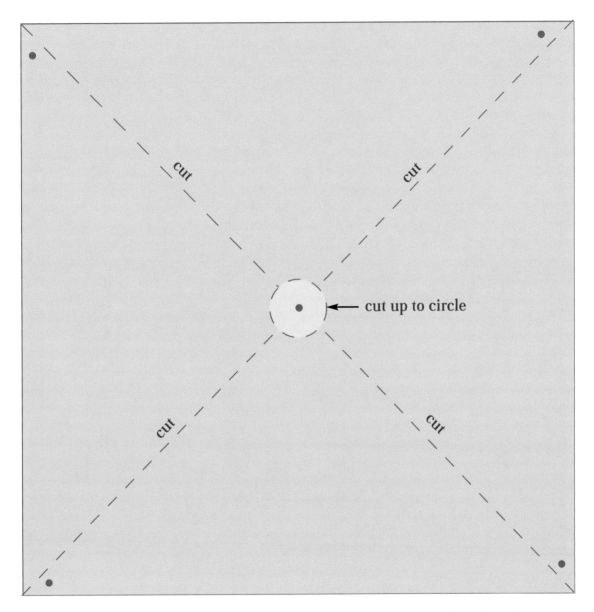

cut up to circle

pinwheel pattern

This pattern can be adjusted to make most any size pinwheel. But keep in mind that if the pinwheel gets too small they are hard to bend. If they are too large they tend to flop too much. After you get good at making the pinwheels, try different papers and sizes to see what you like.

Instead of using fun foam on the front with the pin, use a 3-D sticker.

Try making your pinwheels slightly larger or smaller than the 6-inch size.

Try adding dots of paint to the stick instead of using ribbon.

Let your imagination whirl with some pinwheel variations.

Use decorative-
edged scissors to
cut the edges of
the pinwheel for an
extra-pretty look.

Use the same paper
two different ways.
You can have two
entirely different
looks by switching
which pattern is on
the front and which
is on the back!

what else?

Make pinwheels to use as holiday ornaments. Choose holiday printed papers and instead of using a pin, bead, eraser, and dowel, use a brad or paper fastener to hold the corners in place at the center. The pinwheel won't move but will make a lovely holiday trim. Add a cord for hanging.

Make a pretty centerpiece of pinwheels by placing them in a glass vase filled with pastel jelly beans. Choose paper colors that coordinate with your favorite dishes.

pinwheels

Keep tablecloths from flying in the wind while the breeze moves your pinwheels by placing the pinwheels in a terra cotta pot filled with marbles. Choose deeper colors of paper to match the heaviness of the pot.

If you really want to be creative, use fruit roll ups to make an edible pinwheel! Unroll and put two colors together. Cut in a square. Make the pinwheel as you did for paper, but don't use a pin! Instead the roll up will stick to itself. Add a candy dot in the center.

Glue two pieces of origami paper together, back to back, and then make a pinwheel that becomes an elegant bow. Instead of using a dowel, use a shorter pin and poke through the lid of the box and into an eraser underneath the lid.

painted glass

You don't need to be an artist to paint! Just grab a pencil—glass painting just got easier! With polka-dots (and parts of polka-dots!) your pencil just became your best painting friend.

make it

4

What you need

- New inexpensive pencils with erasers (about 5 to 10 pencils)
- Sharp knife
- Old towel
- Any glass or china item to paint
- Paints made for glass painting
- Disposable plate

Pretty soon you'll have painted polka-dots on all your favorite things.

special tips for this project

- Glass paints come in many brands. Some need to be baked to be dishwasher safe, but most can be air dried and are surprisingly durable. For more information about glass paints, see the Tool Box on page 154.

- This technique works on all kinds of glass and china items. You can paint anything that is china or glass. If the edges are flat it is easier to paint and probably best to start with if you don't have much painting experience.

- If you are painting on something that is purely decorative, you can add glitter while the paint is wet for a fun and sparkling effect.

- This type of painting is so easy to do, you will want everyone in the family to give it a try.

make it

What you do

Gather your painting supplies. You will need the glass paints, diposable plate, an old towel to lay your piece of glass on while you paint, and your painting utensils—which are erasers at the end of pencils! Buy inexpensive pencils with good erasers so you don't feel badly about cutting up the eraser. Remember, paintbrushes can be expensive—so you are really being very frugal! Make a "set" of pencil painters. The first one will be just the flat eraser at the end of the pencil—just the way it comes.

Eraser shapes

1 To make the $\frac{1}{2}$ **eraser pencil painter that works well for making leaves or large petals,** lay the pencil with the eraser on a cutting board. Steady it with your hand or tape it to the board. Use a sharp knife to carefully cut vertically through the top of the eraser about 2/3 down the eraser.

2 **Now use the knife to cut horizontally** through the eraser, meeting where the other cut was made. The piece should be cut through on both sides so you can carefully lift out the piece of eraser. You have just created a half-circle pencil painter!

To make the $^1/_4$ eraser pencil painter that works well for making small petals, cut the $^1/_2$ circle as you did in step 1 and 2. Now cut that $^1/_2$ circle in half making a quarter-circle shape to use as a pencil painter. Make 2 or 3 of each shape so you can switch paint colors without washing the paint from the eraser. The painter erasers actually wash very well, but it is just easier (and more fun!) to have more ready at your fingertips. Now you are ready to paint!

3 Read the directions for the type of paint you are using. Some paints require that you just clean the glass surface and others require that you wipe the surface with a liquid that the manufacturer provides. Follow the instructions given for the type of paint you are using. Plan your design. Practice first on a plain piece of paper. Put a little paint on the disposable plate and dip the eraser that you like into the paint. Carefully dot the paint on the glass piece you have chosen. Repeat until you like your design.

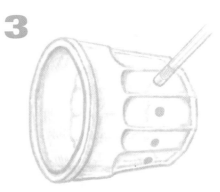

4 Use the half eraser to make leaves or other designs. Use the quarter eraser in the same way. Let the paint dry and follow the manufacturer's instructions for finishing. Sometimes the manufacturer will require that the paint be cured (set for a long time) and then baked. Other paints can air dry without baking. If you are painting dishes that will be used with food BE SURE that the paint is suitable for that purpose. Just read the directions on the paint. Whatever the case, now you can call yourself a glass painter!

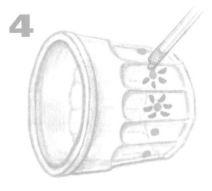

Paint dainty flowers
on a pretty green
vase and fill it with
flowers to match.

Just a few
colorful dots on
this votive holder
makes it more
interesting.

A flat candleholder can also
be used to hold business
cards when it is painted
with pretty designs.

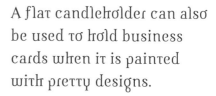

A clear candlestick painted with polka-dots all around and flowers on the base makes a great gift.

Little dots of color bring style to every thing they touch!

Simple dots of different colors make this plain-Jane tumbler look pretty enough to hold some candy sticks or lemonade.

use it

what else?

Use glass paints and the eraser technique to paint all kinds of things. Try painting some china salt and pepper shakers that need a little lift, some glass Christmas ornaments, a vintage cup and saucer that has lost its paint, or even around a window in the kid's playroom.

▲ A vintage sugar bowl found at a flea market takes on a new life with just some dots of color.

painted glass

Pretty candlesticks are decorated with flower-garden-style petals and leaves to make them extra special. The candlesticks can have flat or curved edges because the painting is so easy.

Choose candles in colors and styles that compliment the pretty painted holders.

Just a little painting on the edge of a simple clear-glass plate makes a colorful addition to this pretty tabletop.

the perfect bow

Now you can impress your family and friends with your bow-making know-how! Pick your favorite ribbon, follow a few easy steps, and like magic, you'll have a bow to use on all kinds of things!

make it

5

What you need

- About 5 feet of 1 ½-inch-wide wire-edge ribbon
  (the wider the width of the ribbon the more yardage
  you will need—see the chart on page 43)

- 2 feet of 24 gauge wire

- Scissors to cut ribbon

- Wire snips or old scissors to cut the wire

Make big bows or little bows the very same way—just change the size of the ribbon

special tips for this project

- Wire-edge ribbon works best for this project because it gives the bow body and shape.

- You can use paper ribbon or even fabric ribbon, but the bow will be harder to manage.

- See the Tool box on page 154 for more information about ribbon.

- Wire comes in all weights and colors. Plain 24-gauge wire is inexpensive and comes on a roll or a spool. For more information about wire, see the Tool Box on page 154.

- Save an old pair of scissors to cut wire with for a variety of crafting projects. Mark the scissors using a permanent marker.

- Save your good scissors for cutting ribbon so you get a nice clean edge. Mark these, too, and remind your family that those scissors are for your fine crafting!

make it

What you do

Decide what kind of bow you want to make.
Because there are so many choices when you
purchase ribbon, have in mind the kind of
finished bow you want. If you use wire-edge
ribbon, your bow will stand up better and look
crisper. Non wire-edge ribbon will work as well,
but the finished bow will be limper and more
flowing. Ribbon comes in all widths, patterns, and
styles. If you want to make a small bow, use
narrow ribbon. Even some narrow ribbon comes
with a wire edge. The wider the ribbon the more
yardage you will need. See the table on the
opposite page for approximate lengths of ribbon
based on how wide the ribbon is.

Colored ribbons

1 **Lay the piece of ribbon on a flat surface.**
(These measurements are assuming that you are
using a ribbon that is 1¹/₂ inches wide.) Starting
from the left side of the ribbon, about 12 inches in
from the end, accordion fold the ribbon back and
forth until there are at least four loops on each
side. The 12 inch length that you left on the left
side will be one of the tails. Be sure there are at
least 15 inches of ribbon left on the right side
when you are done making the accordion loops.
That 15 inches will make the center loop and
other tail.

Squeeze the loops together in the middle.
Starting at the center of the 24-inch piece of wire, wind the wire around the center at least 2 times. You should have a length of wire coming up at the top and the bottom after you are done winding the wire in the middle.

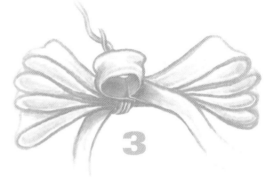

Now this is the tricky (but not difficult) part. Pull the top piece of ribbon to the left and make a loop that looks like a center of a bow right where you wound the wire. Squeeze it in and let the ribbon drape to the bottom right.

Take the bottom wire and wind it around the loop where you squeezed it. Wrap the wire around at least twice. Twist it with the other wire behind the bow to secure the middle loop. Don't trim the wires—you'll need them to attach the bow to a wreath, a package, or wherever your awesome bow is to be used. Pull apart the bow loops to make them the fullness that you like. Trim the ends of the ribbons the length you want. You can cut them straight or notch them by folding each end in half the long way and cutting a V notch. However you trim it, you just made a beautiful bow!

Approximate Ribbon Yardages to Make a Bow

$1/2$-inch-wide ribbon = 4 feet ($1\frac{1}{3}$ yards)

1-inch-wide ribbon = 7 feet ($2\frac{1}{3}$ yards)

$1\frac{1}{2}$-inch-wide ribbon = 9 feet (3 yards)

2-inch-wide ribbon = 12 feet (4 yards)

$2\frac{1}{2}$-inch-wide ribbon = 15 feet (5 yards)

3-inch-wide ribbon = 18 feet (6 yards)

Show off
your bow -
making skill
by putting
bows
everywhere!

Add a beautiful
piece of vintage
jewelry to the
center of a
colorful plaid bow.

A wide-striped
ribbon makes a
fun and
graphic bow.

Choose wide ribbons with
plenty of shine to make
bows for banisters and
wreaths at holiday time.

String jingle bells
on the wire and
then tie some small
wisps of finer
golden ribbon
around the middle.

Notch the end of
the bow tail by
folding it in half
and then cutting a
V-shaped notch.

Add stickers that
you love or that
spell special
initials to the tails
of your pretty bow.

45

what else?

Make bows to use on top of packages, of course. But now you also know how to make a bow to attach to a napkin ring, to add to a little girl's headband, to tie back curtains, to brighten up a picture frame, to decorate an outside door, and to add to a pretty wreath.

▲ Add even more sparkle to a purchased fall wreath. This pretty bow was made using a 1-inch-wide ribbon. We pinned a vintage brooch to the center of the bow.

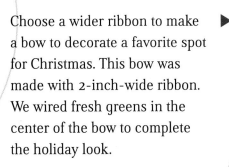

perfect bow

Dress up any party cake with a beautiful bow on top. Try using a tone-on-tone white ribbon for a shower or wedding cake or a pretty pastel ribbon for a special birthday topper.

Choose a wider ribbon to make a bow to decorate a favorite spot for Christmas. This bow was made with 2-inch-wide ribbon. We wired fresh greens in the center of the bow to complete the holiday look.

classy
millefiori clay

Fashioned after the
beautiful glassware of
"many flowers" this
polymer clay version is
so easy and fun to
make—the look can be
classic or simply playful
and full of fun.

make it

6

What you need

- Eight colors (or more) of polymer clay such as Sculpey or Fimo

- Waxed paper

- Rolling pin

- Sharp knife

- Tool for making a hole in the clay such as a toothpick or awl

- Cookie sheet

- Aluminum foil

- Oven

Don't worry if the clay pieces aren't perfect— that is the beauty of handmade items.

special tips for this project

❋ Polymer clay usually comes in little wrapped squares and in many brands and many colors. Choose the kind that you like to work with. Look at the Tool Box on page 154 for some tips on polymer clay.

❋ You will need to work the clay well with your hands before you roll it out. The softer the clay, the easier it is to mold into the shapes you want. Store the leftover clay in small plastic bags.

❋ The beauty of using this clay is that you can control the colors and shapes that you like. Do not expect the clay projects to look perfect— they should look handmade. The colors will blend slightly as you roll and manipulate the clay. Enjoy the new colors that are made!

❋ Because you are working with small pieces of clay, you keep the scale of your finished pieces small as well. Beads are a perfect end use for these projects as well as small ornaments and trims.

make it

Cut off a little piece of each color of clay you want to use. You will need 7 (or more) colors for the inside canes and 1 color for wrapping the canes. Set each color on a piece of waxed paper.

1 Use your hands to form each of the seven pieces of clay into a long thin cane. Make one of each color of cane. You can make them any size you want depending on how big you want your finished pieces to be. A good size is about $1/4$-inch in diameter and about 4 inches long. Set the other block of clay to be used for the outside layer aside.

2 Stack the canes together by putting one in the middle and the others all the way around the center one. Gently make them stick together but try not to blend the colors too much.

Clay pieces

3 **Now roll out the outside layer** with the rolling pin. If you made the canes 4 inches long, then make the rectangle 4 inches wide and long enough to wrap around the canes. Roll it out to be about $^1/_4$-inch thick. Trim the ends with a sharp knife to even them.

4 **Lay the stacked inside canes** on the rolled out piece of clay. Roll the outside piece around the canes. Use your fingers or knife to smooth the edges where it seals. To make the pieces all feel like one solid unit, roll the entire piece back and forth to make a nice smooth cylinder.

5 **Use the knife to slice off pieces** of the pretty millefiori. If you want, use the rolling pin to roll the piece thinner—this will change the shapes of the inside pieces. Or you can leave the slices as they are and just smooth the edges.

Cover the cookie sheet with foil and lay the pieces on the foil to get ready to bake them.

Now you are ready to bake the clay. Be sure to read the manufacturer's instructions carefully. Different brands of polymer clay have slightly different baking directions. If you are planning to make an ornament, necklace, or anything with a hole in it, be sure to make a hole with a toothpick, awl, or knife before you bake it. Bake as directed. After it is baked, let it cool and add glitter or whatever you like. How beautiful!

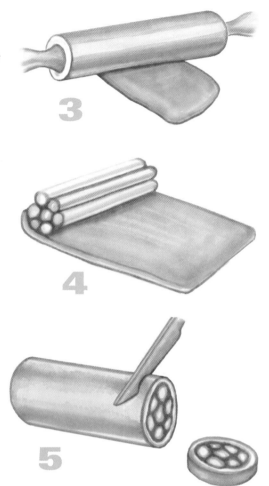

Make millefiori beads that string easily on beading wire—then add some tiny purchased beads to string along with them.

Form the clay slice into a little heart to give to someone special.

Pretty shapes and lots of color make these little projects full of fun.

Make larger shapes and dust with glitter after baking to use for sparkling light pulls.

Make a pretty little necklace by adding a thin strip of clay around the millefiori slice and looping the strip at the top. Glue some micro-mini beads to the edge after it is baked.

Clay buttons lend a handmade look to any favorite sweater. Be sure to remove the buttons before washing the sweater.

Let the kids help make these tiny and fun-to-make beads. Be sure to make the hole in each bead before baking them.

53

use it

what else?

Little bits of colored clay combine to make so many pretty things. Use this millefiori idea to make a vintage-looking paperweight. Make the bottom as for the coaster. Trim the edges and then add the glass dome top. The glass tops are available at crafts and hobby stores.

▲ Combine the slices of your pretty clay into a circle shape. Gently roll it out to be a little thinner and larger. Bake it and use for a handy coaster.

54

millefiori clay

◀ Lay six of your millefiori slices together. Use a knife to blend the clay edges so they stay together. Add a little wire loop in the top before it is baked. Then add a pretty ribbon afterwards to make a lovely ornament.

Make two tiny little pieces of millefiori in your favorite colors. Put the two pieces together and form into a square. Be sure to make the hole in the corner before it is baked. After it is baked, add a little glue and glitter, put a ribbon in the hole, and use as a pretty and colorful necklace. ▶

lacey snowflakes

So easy to make, yet always full of wonder, this paper version of a favorite wintertime shape is fun for the whole family.

make it

7

What you need

- Tracing paper (unless you plan to photocopy the patterns)

- 7x7-inch square of lightweight to medium-weight paper (the square can be any size—but this size works well when you are learning)

- Pencil

- Scissors

- Iron (optional)

Soon you'll have pretty snowflakes decorating every corner of your house.

special tips for this project

❄ Snowflakes can be made out of most any lightweight paper—even tissue paper. If the paper gets too heavy, it is hard to fold and cut.

❄ Even though we usually think of paper snowflakes made with a white or solid-colored paper, try a patterned paper for a different look.

❄ Use good quality paper-cutting scissors for this project. It is difficult to cut through multiple layers of paper using poor scissors.

❄ We have given patterns on page 59 for some of the snowflakes shown in this chapter. It is so easy to make your own patterns. Look at simple shapes you might see around the house (such as cookie cutter shapes) to give you ideas for the shapes you cut out.

make it

What you do

Decide what kind of paper you want to use.
Be sure the paper isn't too heavy or it will be hard to cut. Cut the paper into the square size that you want. If you are using the patterns, opposite, cut the paper to fit that size or enlarge the patterns to fit your paper. Trace or photocopy the pattern if you are choosing to use one we have provided.

Fold the paper in half. Crease the edges with the edge of your fingernail.

Fold the paper in half again. Crease the edges of the new folds with the edge of your fingernail. This will make it easier to cut the folded paper.

Bring down the top left corner to make a triangle. Crease the edges. You will be cutting on the folded edges and on the ends. If you are using a pattern, draw around it on your folded paper.

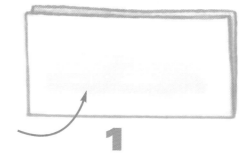

Cut notches or shapes from the folded sides and outside edge. Cut on the lines, following the lines that you drew from the patterns. Or, make V cuts or any shapes you like. Open up the snowflake. If necessary, put the paper snowflake between two pieces of clean white paper and with a cool iron, iron the snowflake. This will take out the creases. Just be sure to keep the iron cool so it doesn't burn the paper. Look at your pretty winter snowflake!

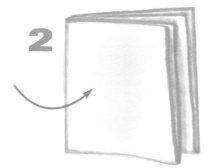

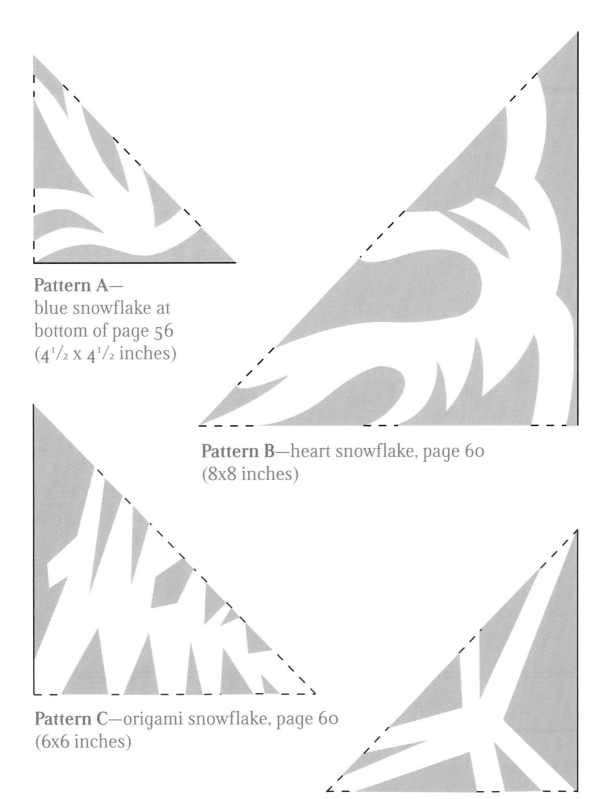

Pattern A—
blue snowflake at
bottom of page 56
($4^1/_2$ x $4^1/_2$ inches)

Pattern B—heart snowflake, page 60
(8x8 inches)

Pattern C—origami snowflake, page 60
(6x6 inches)

Pattern D—star snowflake, page 61
($5^1/_2$ x $5^1/_2$ inches)

Snowflake Patterns
(the dark areas are the areas to be cut out)

Try origami paper to make a beautifully unusual snowflake. Use pattern C on page 59.

Simple stripes on a patterned piece of paper make an optical illusion.

Use pattern B on page 59 to make this snowflake.

Don't forget to cut the outside edges with shapes (as well as the folded sides) to get an interesting outside edge on your finished snowflake.

Use pattern D on page 59 to make this star-shaped snowflake.

Make your own snowflake style—no two are alike!

use it

▲ Layer large snowflakes just as they would fall as a centerpiece table liner. Choose colors that match or coordinate with the vase you are using.

snowflakes

◀ Use the finished snowflake as a stencil and paint a design on a handmade greeting card. Just place the snowflake stencil on the card and with a dotting motion, lightly paint the open spaces. Any acrylic or craft paint designed for paper will work. Use silver paint on a white card for a wintry look.

Cut a snowflake out of tissue paper and put it between two glass plates to make a lacey look for a fancy luncheon. We used hot pink tissue paper to make the snowflake and put it between two clear pink plates. ▶

stylish posies

You'll be picking these posies to go everywhere— on hats, coats, tabletops or anywhere you want a touch of spring.

make it

8

What you need

- Tracing paper
- Pencil
- Scissors
- Two 12-inch squares of medium to heavy weight fabric
- 12-inch square of fusible bonding
- Iron
- 24-gauge wire; wire cutters or old scissors to cut wire
- Strong glue such as E6000

Try printed fabrics as well as solids to make some pretty fabric posies.

special tips for this project

❈ Any fabric will work for these posies, but a medium to heavier weight fabric with some body works best. Some fabrics that work well are brushed corduroy, heavy cottons, and lightweight upholstery fabrics.

❈ Fusible bonding is almost a magical way of fusing two pieces of fabric together. It can be found at crafts or fabric stores. For more information about this great product, see the Tool Box on page 154.

❈ The wire in the petals makes them stand up and appear more real. You can leave out the wire and have your flower be more limp-looking and softer if you choose.

❈ Try adding some interesting beads or other centers to the flowers when you are done making them. It will make them look more real and add a touch of 3-D fun.

make it

What you do

Prepare your fabric. You are going to make the fabric stronger by fusing two pieces together. Place the two pieces of fabric with wrong sides together. Now slip the piece of bonding between them. Using a medium setting on the iron, iron the pieces together. Now they will appear to be one piece of fabric. You will use this method of preparing your fabric no matter how you plan to make your flower.

Next, choose the posies you want to make. We are showing *three* ways to make the flowers and giving you lots of petals and shapes to choose from. The first way is to glue the petals to a large base piece. The second way is to start the first layer by gluing the petals to a small square. Using the large base

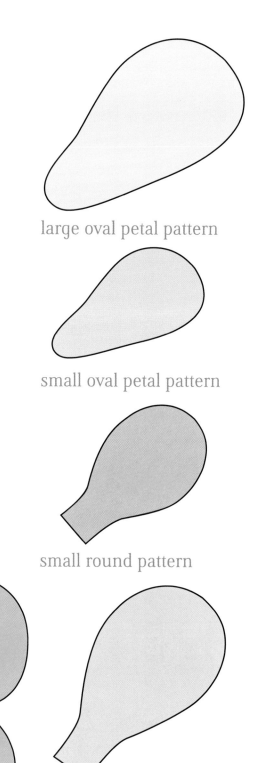

large oval petal pattern

small oval petal pattern

small round pattern

large round pattern

large flower base pattern

center square pattern

66

piece first makes a stronger base and is best for larger flowers. Gluing the petals to a small square works well for the smaller flowers and gives the flower a looser appearance. The third way to make these pretty posies is to layer three larger shapes to look more like a tropical flower. (Tropical patterns are on page 68.) You'll want to try all three ways to get different looks for your flowers.

However you want to make the flowers, trace or photocopy the patterns that you want to use. Cut out the patterns. Now trace around them onto the fabric that you prepared. You can use as many petals as you like on each flower until you get the fullness you like. You will probably need about 8 large and 8 small petals for each flower plus the base if you are using the individual petals.

1 **Cut a piece of wire about 2 inches long** using wire cutters or old scissors. Carefully open up the petal that you fused and lay the wire inside. Iron the petal shut again. It will rebond and keep the wire inside! Do this on all of the petals. If you are using the tropical pattern, lay the wires on each of the petals on the larger piece and then rebond.

2 **Using the little square or the flower base,** use the strong glue to start gluing the petals in a circle. They don't need to overlap.

3 **Glue them until you have one layer.** Then start the second layer using some big and small petals. Start a third layer with just small petals. If you are using the tropical patterns, just layer the patterns.

4 **For the top layer of petals,** turn back the end and glue it so the end doesn't show. Do this for all of the top petals. Let the glue dry. Arrange the petals any way you want to make them seem real. The wire inside will let you move them into very realistic shapes. You just made a pretty posies!

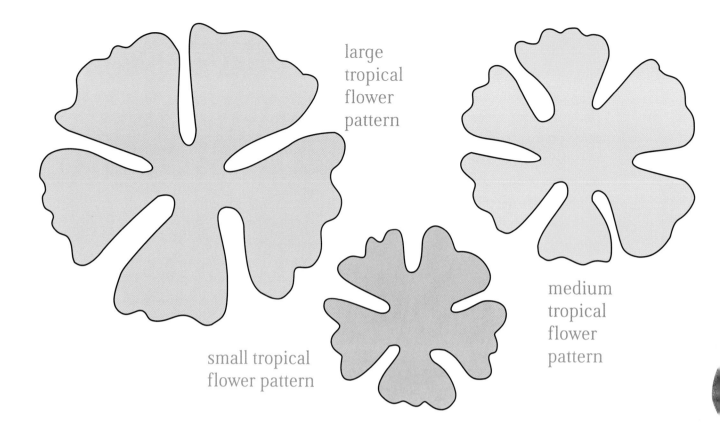

large
tropical
flower
pattern

medium
tropical
flower
pattern

small tropical
flower pattern

Add a center to your
flower using little beads
or colored pearls to make
the flower seem even
more real.

Using rich brown tones and
adding a textured button
can make your tropical
flower pattern seem like a
country fall beauty.

This flower was made using the square base, and using all the same size petals for a different look.

A heavy red cotton fabric works great to make this bright tropical beauty.

This bright patterned fabric makes a fun flower. We added a little green leaf to the back of the flower by cutting a leaf-shape and gluing it to the back.

Make a pretty posies for everyone you know. They'll love you for it!

use it

what else?

These flowers will make everything they touch seem happier. Put one on a package, put another on a barrette. Use a small one for an elegant lapel pin, or add one to a curtain tie back. Glue them to a wreath form for a beautiful flowered wreath, or just give one to a special friend.

▲ Dress up a favorite purse by clipping a pretty purple flower to the purse handle or buckle. This flower was made using the big flower base and brushed purple corduroy.

A pretty straw hat is the perfect place to put a big, red, fashion flower that you made from textured fabric. Add a band of ribbon if you'd like to make the hat one-of-a-kind.

Use bright colors of warm-toned fabric to make a flower for a spring tabletop trim. Add a single green leaf and glue the flower to a matching ribbon. Tie the pretty posies on a sage-green napkin.

clever cones

Fill them with candy, flowers, ornaments, jewelry or any other unexpected treat—your simple cone makes the perfect holder for most anything.

make it

What you need

- Tracing paper; pencil
- 7x7-inch piece of cardstock paper
- Scissors (regular and decorative)
- Tacky crafts glue
- Clothespin
- Paper punch
- 12-inch length of cord or fine ribbon

Once you get started making these, you'll think of all kinds of ways to use them!

special tips for this project

❋ We have given you two pattern sizes to make the cone. Choose the one that fits your project idea. Use a sturdy paper to make the cone if you are going to fill it with candy or other heavy items. Thinner paper will work, too, but it will not keep its shape as well.

❋ Add things to your cone to make it fit your project needs. For example, trim with rickrack or pompoms for a May basket, or with gold parchment for a more elegant look.

❋ Look for more information about the other supplies on this list, in the Tool Box section on page 154. It will give you tips on where to find the products you need.

make it

What you do

1 **Trace the cone pattern, opposite,** onto tracing paper or photocopy it. If you use tracing paper be sure to mark the dotted line and the dots for holes. Cut out the pattern and trace around it onto the paper you have chosen. Be sure to mark the dotted line and holes again on the printed paper. (If you can find paper that is printed with a pattern on both sides, that is great. That way the inside and the outside of the cone both look interesting.) Cut out the cone. Punch the holes where the dots are on the pattern.

2 **Carefully bend the paper** around, curving the paper into a cone shape. Sometimes you might have to readjust the point to make it fit perfectly. Run a bead of glue along the edge of the cone and overlap to line it up with the dotted line. Use a clothespin to hold the cone together while the glue dries.

3 **Tie a knot in one end of the cord or ribbon.** Starting from the outside of the cone, thread the ribbon or cording through one of the holes and then inside the other hole. Pull the knot tight up to the first side hole.

4 **Adjust the length of the cording** or ribbon to the length you want for the handle and tie a knot on the other side. Trim the ends of the ribbon. Add any other trims you like using the crafts glue. You just made a dainty little cone to fill with goodies of all kinds!

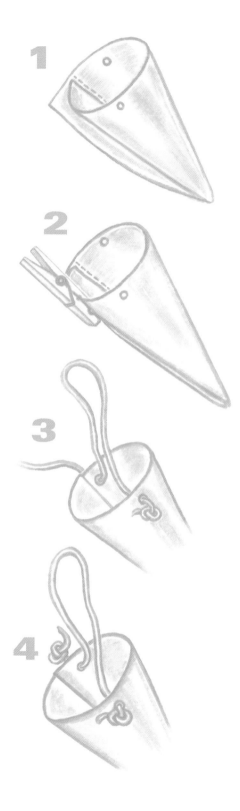

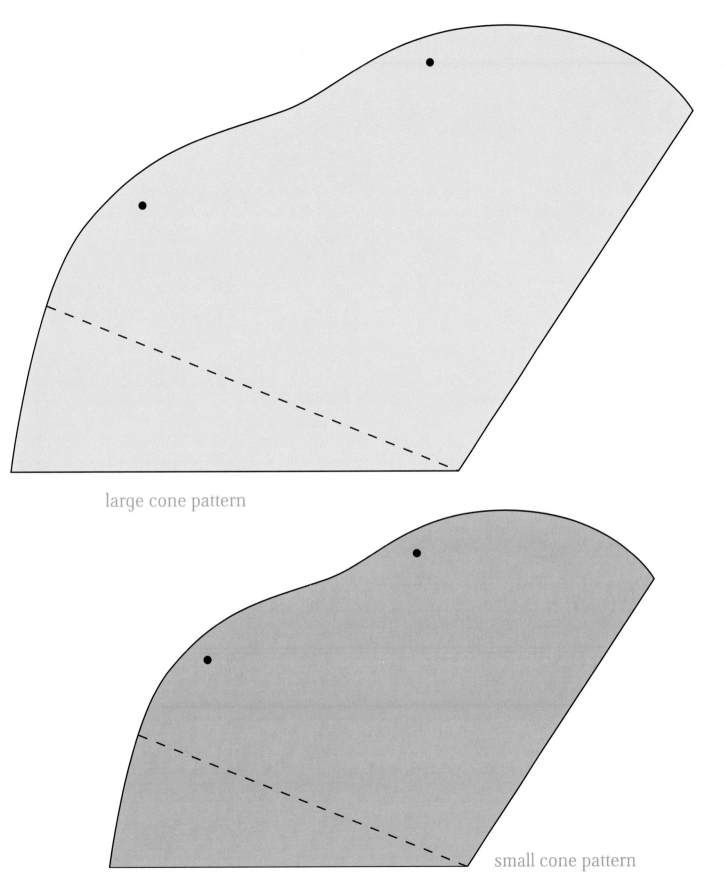

large cone pattern

small cone pattern

75

You'll be making these cones by the dozens and trimming them to fit your style.

Use two strands of ribbon and tie a knot at the ends to hold the two pieces together.

Put one bright cone inside another, add a graphic ribbon, and you've created a fun and contemporary look.

76

Printed ribbon and pompoms make this cone pretty as you please.

Use decorative-edge scissors to cut the top edge of the cone for an extra-pretty look.

Papers that are printed on both sides make the inside and the outside of the cone full of fun.

Cut a cone from a paper doily and layer it on top of the one you made. Choose a lacey ribbon handle.

use it

what else?

Make a one-of-a-kind art cone. Cut out the cone from lightweight cardstock and have the children draw their sweet artwork on the paper. Use a bright colored ribbon as a hanger. These little cones will become works of art and can hold small art supplies or other treasures.

▲ Make a pretty table favor for a baby shower using pink and blue papers. Add a little colored tissue inside and fill with jelly beans.

◀ Welcome any visitor by decorating a doorknob with a little striped cone. Fill the cone with unexpected items such as candy or tiny fruits.

Make a pretty little cone using a metallic foil paper. Make another cone from gold parchment and fit it inside the first cone. Trim the edge with decorative scissors and dust with glitter. Fill the cone with tiny gold ornaments for a clever holiday tree trim. ▶

fabric yo-yos

Tiny pieces of fabric gather up to make the sweetest little circles of color to use in all kinds of ways.

make it

10

What you need

- Tracing paper (you will need this unless you plan to photocopy the patterns)
- Pencil
- Small scraps of fabric
- Scissors
- Needle
- Strong sewing thread or quilting thread

Use up little scraps of fabric by making these cute yo-yos.

special tips for this project

Fabric yo-yos can be made from almost any fabric. You can use cottons, silks, wool, even felt. For more information about fabrics in general, see the Tool Box on page 154.

Use a strong thread such as quilting thread to make the yo-yos or use a double regular sewing thread. See the Tool Box on page 154 for tips about sewing threads.

Stitching the yo-yos together after they are made is just a matter of taking a stitch where you want them to connect. This is done after all of the yo-yos are made. You can stitch them together at the sides to make large flat items such as pillow covers or table squares. Or you can stack them to use as package toppers or curtain tie-backs.

Think of other things that you can add to the yo-yos after they are stitched such as buttons or pins.

make it

What you do

Cut fabric circles you need to make the yo-yo.
Using tracing paper, trace around the circle
pattern you want to use or photocopy it. Use one
of the patterns on the opposite page or just make
your own circle. Remember that the circle will
become quite a bit smaller when you make it into
a yo-yo. The diameter of the finished circle will be
half the size of the circle of fabric you start with.
For example, for a 1-inch finished yo-yo, you will
need a 2-inch circle. Draw around the circle onto
the fabric that you have chosen. Cut out the circle.

1 **Thread the needle.** Tie a knot at the end of the
thread. Turn under a scant $\frac{1}{4}$ inch of fabric as
you work running stitches close to the folded
edge. Don't make the stitches too tiny or the hole
of the yo-yo will be too big. Make the stitches
about $\frac{1}{4}$ inch apart.

2 **Continue to sew all around the circle** until you
have come back to where you started sewing.
The yo-yo will flatten out a bit and curl up on the
edges. Bring the needle out to the side without the
cut edge.

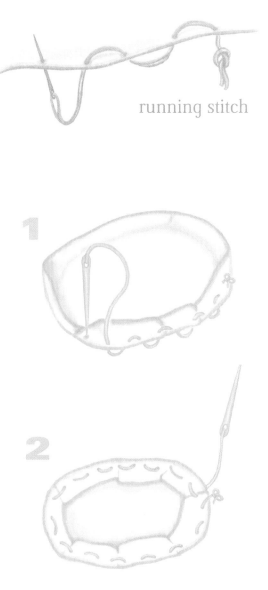

running stitch

1

2

3 **Pull the needle firmly** to gather up the stitches and draw the yo-yo closed. The yo-yo will bunch up and become 3-D. Take a few more little stitches where the thread comes out to hold the yo-yo in place.

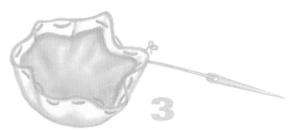

4 **Adjust the gathers in the the yo-yo and flatten it down.** Add any embellishments you like, such as a button, pin, or another small yo-yo on top. You just made a cute little yo-yo!

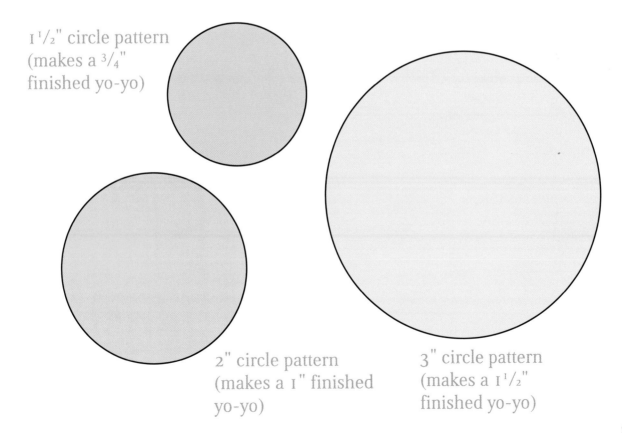

1 1/2" circle pattern (makes a 3/4" finished yo-yo)

2" circle pattern (makes a 1" finished yo-yo)

3" circle pattern (makes a 1 1/2" finished yo-yo)

Use vintage fabrics and overlap yo-yos of different sizes.

Make a cute little hair accessory by stacking two yo-yos on top of one another. Glue a clip or barrette to the back.

Lightweight felt or upholstery fabrics can be used to make large-sized yo-yos.

Stitch them and stack them— make some yo-yo fun.

Stack pretty pink yo-yos and use them as a bow on a little girl's special package.

Use two different prints of the same color family and stack them together.

Layer two yo-yos and sew a button to the center of the pretty stack.

Stack yo-yos made from rich golden fabric colors and then add a favorite jewelry pin or other vintage piece to make an interesting 3-D look.

use it

what else?

Use pretty fabric yo-yos for all kinds of things—glue them to barrettes to put in your little girl's hair, sew them to the edge of a kitchen towel to dress up your kitchen, or add them to a pretty package for a best friend. Use fabric yo-yos any place you want a little touch of 3-D fabric fun.

▲ Make three very tiny yo-yos from satin fabric and sew them into the corner of a pretty cloth napkin for a sweet tabletop accent. Fold a tiny piece of ribbon and stitch under the yo-yo to create a little leaf.

fabric yo-yos

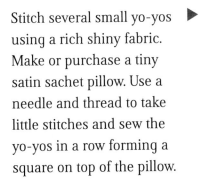

◄ Make three yo-yos the sizes you like. Sew a pretty button in the middle of each one and sew them in a row on a colorful ribbon. Tie the ribbon around a curtain or drape to make a clever tie-back.

Stitch several small yo-yos using a rich shiny fabric. Make or purchase a tiny satin sachet pillow. Use a needle and thread to take little stitches and sew the yo-yos in a row forming a square on top of the pillow. ▶

tissue paper flowers

Light and airy and full of color, these beautiful blooms look like real tropical beauties. Make them for anywhere and everywhere you want a touch of almost-natural beauty.

make it

11

What you need

- Tracing paper (you will need this unless you plan to photocopy the patterns)
- Tissue paper (at least three different colors)
- Pencil
- Scissors
- Paper punch
- Green chenille stem
- Green floral tape
- White tacky crafts glue

Try all kinds of tissue-paper combinations— even printed papers!

special tips for this project

* Tissue paper comes in all colors and styles. For more information about this fun kind of paper, see the Tool Box on page 154.

* The old name for chenille stem is pipe cleaner. They are really the same thing except that now chenille stems come in all kinds of colors and styles. They're not for cleaning pipes anymore! See the Tool Box on page 154 for more information about these.

* Green floral tape is used by florists but can be purchased at crafts stores as well. It stretches and hides all kinds of mistakes. See the Tool Box on page 154.

* You can make the flowers quite full by using lots of layers of tissue paper or less full by using fewer layers. If you use too many layers, it will be hard to keep them on the stem with the floral tape. Just add a drop of glue if you need to.

make it

What you do

First, decide on the colors of paper you want to use.
Three shades of the same color works well with the
center circle a different color such as green. But any
colors will work. Flowers come in all colors!

Trace or photocopy the center and petal patterns,
opposite, and cut them out. Trace around the patterns
onto the tissue paper and cut out. You will need about
2-5 centers and 2-5 petals of each color depending on
how full you want your flower to be. Be sure to cut the
slits in the center circle pieces as shown on the
pattern. Punch a hole in the center of each petal and
center. Because the paper is so thin, you can group
them together and punch several at once. Set the
tissue pieces aside.

Coil one end of the chenille stem. This will keep the
tissue center and petals from falling off. Starting from
the bottom of the stem, bring all of the center pieces
up almost to the top of the stem near the curl.

Now, starting with the smallest petals, bring all of the
pieces up from the bottom until you have used all of
the pieces. Make the petals turn different ways. Don't
keep them straight.

Pinch all the tissue pieces together at the bottom of
the flower. It will seem strange to crush the tissue
enough to do this, but the wrinkles in the tissue will
make it look more real. While you are holding the
flower with one hand, place one end of the floral tape
over the tissue and start wrapping and pulling the
tape. The tape is meant to stretch and will only stick if
it is pulled at the same time. Wrap the entire stem. Cut
off the remaining tape. Add a dot of glue at the bottom
to secure the floral tape. Pull the petals out and fluff
the flower. So pretty!

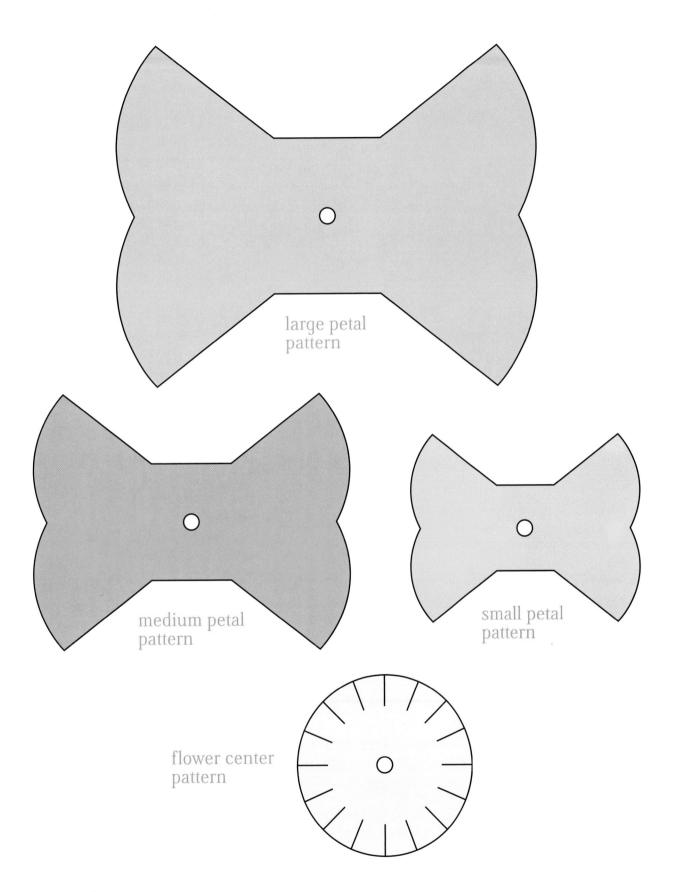

large petal
pattern

medium petal
pattern

small petal
pattern

flower center
pattern

Pinking shears or decorative-edge scissors make the flowers have an uneven and beautifully natural-looking feel.

Periwinkle tissue with a lime green center makes this flower bright and beautiful.

Pick your favorite colors to make the freshest of tissue paper blooms.

Use one color for the center of the flower and then use different hues of the same color for the outside petals for a monochromatic look.

Use some polka-dot paper to make some of the petals for a fun flower surprise.

Try an all-white version of this flower and use a silver stem for an elegant look.

use it

what else?

You'll want these beautiful flowers everywhere. Wear these flowers in your hair, pin one to a pretty jacket, make a bouquet in the bride's colors and use as favors at the wedding dinner, group them in large vases, or give one wrapped in cellophane as a special thank you.

▲ For a beautiful name card holder, make a flower in glorious colors and cut a leaf from green vellum paper. Write the name of the guest on the leaf and place the flower and leaf on the plate.

When serving a fresh summer drink, add a pretty flower to the serving pitcher. Wind the stem around the handle of the pitcher and place on a tray with glasses of pink lemonade or punch.

These flowers look so real, ▶ you could display them in pretty vases. Choose three colors of vases and find tissue colors to closely match the vase colors. Don't put the colors that match in the vases—switch them around to make a pleasing grouping.

hand-dipped candles

There is nothing to it—just dip your own beautiful candles and you'll light up your decorating scheme in no time!

make it

12

What you need

- Candle wax (new or use old candles)
- Sharp knife
- Old saucepan
- Old can (such as an empty vegetable can)
- Heat source such as a stove or hot plate (Do not use microwave!)
- Waxed paper
- Candle wicking
- Candle coloring and scent (optional)
- Bowl or deep pan of ice water

What a great way to use up old candles— make pretty new ones!

special tips for this project

❀ Candle-making supplies can be found at crafts and most discount stores in the crafts section. See the Tool Box on page 154 for specific information about all the kinds of candle supplies you can buy including wax, wicking, scent, color, and more.

❀ Use old pans and bowls. You probably won't be able to clean them up well enough to use for anything else.

❀ This is a messy (but fun) project so cover surfaces well.

❀ You can add any color or scent you like by using purchased products designed for just that reason or you can use pieces of old crayons or colored candles.

make it

What you do

Prepare the candle wax.
Candle wax comes in big, clear, no-color slabs or sometimes in smaller colored chunks. If you are starting with a large pieces, cut them into smaller chunks (about ½ to 1-inch pieces) with a knife. Put the chunks into the old can. You can also use old candles—just cut them up and put them into the old can. (If you can't get the old wick out of the old candle, don't worry. When the wax melts, the wick will float in the wax and you can take it out.) You can make any color candles that you like. It is fun to have more than one color heating at once so you can dip into more than one color at a time. That, of course, will require more than one can and one saucepan.

Candle pieces

Fill the saucepan about ½ full of water.
Put the can of chunked candle wax in the saucepan of water. Put the pan on the stove. The water will boil and melt the wax in the can. Don't let the water boil too hard. It should just simmer and slowly melt the wax. NEVER put the wax directly on the stove or in the microwave. It is very flammable. After the wax is melted, add any coloring or scent you want. For color you can use a purchased product or put bits of old crayons or bits of old candle pieces in the wax. Turn off the stove. If you are using more than one color you will need more than one saucepan and more than one can.

Cover the work area with waxed paper. Use a potholder and lift the can out of the water and onto the waxed paper. Put the bowl of ice water beside the can of wax.

2 Cut a piece of candle wicking the size you want. You will be making two candles at a time. A good length to start with is about 16 inches long. The length can vary a lot. You will need some extra to hold on to when you are dipping the candles. Dip each end of the wicking into the wax and then quickly take them out, keeping the two candles separated.

3 Immediately dip each end of the waxed wicking into the ice water. The wax will cool quickly and start to build up on the wicking. Repeat back and forth quickly between wax and water. The ice water will set the wax almost immediately so you can move back and forth from the can to the bowl very quickly,

4 After the wax has built up enough, (about 4 or 5 times), you can alternate and have one side in wax while the other side is in water. As the candles get bigger, this will keep them from sticking together.

When the candles are the size you like them, hang them over a chair back or rack to dry. After they are completely dry (this will only take a few minutes) cut them apart so you can use each one. Slice off the bottom of the base to even it off so it will fit more easily into a candle holder. Wow, you just made real candles!

Note: Because the bases of these hand-dipped candles will not be flat, be sure the candles are level and secure before lighting them. You may hear a popping sound when they are lit. This is just a little water that might be trapped between layers. Remember, never leave a burning candle unattended.

Add your own contemporary style to this old-fashioned way of making candles.

Try making stripes on the candles by dipping them in one color for the first 5 or 6 times and then finishing them by dipping them in a complimentary color.

The bumps and imperfections of these candles make them look wonderfully handmade.

These long candles are a cousin to a purchased taper— but with more personality.

Use more than one color of wax when you dip the candles. Slicing off the bottom of the candle will make it level and reveal the cool colors.

Candles can be short or tall. These little candles will fit in a votive candle holder.

After the candle is dipped and cooled, add a design to the side by slicing a little section off to reveal the layers of color inside.

use it

what else?

❄ Don't cut the candles apart. Instead, drape them over a door knob or peg for an old fashioned look.

❄ Wrap a pretty candle holder in a box. Criss-cross a set of your handmade candles and tie them to the package for an unexpected surprise.

▲ Dip the candles in more than one color of wax to fit the look of a favorite holiday.

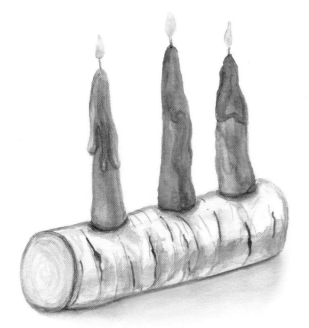

◀ A birthday cupcake will look even more special with a handmade candle in the middle. Place a bit of waxed paper over the bottom of the candle before putting it into the cupcake or use a birthday candle holder.

Secure the candles on a glass tray and then fill the tray with tiny seeds or beans that compliment the colors of the candles. ▼

Use a pretty piece of wood as a ▲ showcase for these natural- looking candles. Just drill holes in the wood and put the candles in the holes. How pretty.

103

ribbon roses

Beautiful ribbon roses can be created anytime of year and you can have them in every glorious color you wish! Just pick the colors that you love and you'll have them by the dozen before you know it!

make it

13

What you need

- 6-inch piece of 1-inch-wide ribbon for rose center (wire-edge or non wire-edge)

- 12-inch piece of 1-inch-wide ribbon for outside petals (wire-edge or non wire-edge ribbon)

- 3-inch piece of green ribbon for rose leaf

- 1 yard of 24 gauge wire

- Scissors to cut ribbon

- Wire snips or old scissors to cut wire

- Green floral tape

Don't forget to try plaid and polka-dot ribbons!

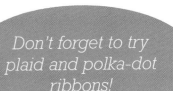

special tips for this project

❀ The wider the ribbon you choose, the larger the rose bloom. 1-inch wide ribbon works well. Anything wider than 1 1/2 inches gets a little too large and hard to handle.

❀ You can use non wire-edge ribbon or wire-edge ribbon to make the roses. Either one works well. Just follow the directions that fit the type of ribbon you choose.

❀ Mix the colors of ribbon if you like. Making the inside and outside petals different colors makes the rose seem more realistic looking.

❀ For more information about wire and floral tape, see the Tool Box on page 154.

make it

What you do

Ribbon comes in all kinds of colors, fiber content, weight, and width. It comes wire-edge or non wire- edge. Most any ribbon about 1-inch wide will work for these roses. Follow the instructions for the type of ribbon that you choose.

First, make the center of the rose. You will make this the same way whether you are using wire-edge ribbon or non wire-edge ribbon.

Lay the 6 inch length of ribbon out and start rolling it from one end. If the edges looked frayed just fold them under.

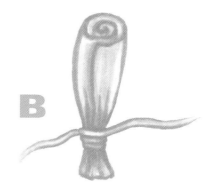

Cut an 8-inch length of wire. Pinch one end of the rolled up ribbon together and coil the wire tightly around the bottom edge. Leave a tail of wire at both ends. Set aside.

Now you are ready to make the petals of the rose. If you are using non wire-edge ribbon:
Lay out a piece of ribbon about 8 to 12 inches long, depending on how full you want your rose to be. Cut a piece of wire about 12 inches long. Starting at the bottom edge and at the end of the ribbon, weave the wire in and out of the ribbon as if working the running stitch. (See page 10.) Some ribbons are easy to poke through and some are not. Make the wire "stitches" about 1/2-inch apart.

Gather the ribbon into the center of the wire.

3 Lay the center of the rose that you made at one end of the gathered ribbon. Twist the tail of the rose center wire with the wire from the gathered ribbon. Roll up the rose twisting the wire as you go until the ribbon is used up.

4 Secure the base of the rose by wrapping it with wire. Twist the extra wires together to form a stem if desired, or cut the wire. Trim the ends of the 3-inch piece of green ribbon and put a hole in the center for a leaf if desired. Wrap the entire stem with floral tape if you like. For tips on using floral tape, see page 90.

1 If you are using wire-edge ribbon:
Cut about an 8-inch length of ribbon. Carefully pull (from both sides) the wire that is already in the ribbon. It is usually a very thin wire, but easy to pull. Just be sure you pull from both sides to gather the ribbon or you will pull it out. Add the center of the rose as you did for the non-wire edge ribbon as in step 3.

2 To make a leaf without a stem, use a small piece of wire to cinch in the small leaf made from the 3-inch piece of green ribbon. Twist the wires together from the rose and leaf to hold them together. Trim the leaf ends if you like. You just made a beautiful rose!

These roses started as variegated wire-edge ribbon and soon became a glorious cluster of naturally looking shaded roses.

Copper colored ribbon winds around to make this shiny metallic looking rose.

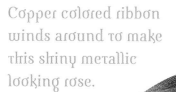

This hot pink satin ribbon did not have a wire edge. Trimmed with floral tape, it looks like a long stem beauty.

Created to stand alone or in bouquets, these life-like posies are sure to make you smile.

Combining a center of red and outside petals of soft pink, this rose is oh-so-beautiful. Both are wire-edge ribbons.

Polka-dot ribbon makes this rose full of fun. Add a stem to make it seem magically real.

Satin non wire-edge ribbon in two colors makes this stand-alone beauty a real winner. The bloom sets on a variegated green ribbon leaf.

use it

what else?

Make ribbon roses to decorate gift bags or boxes. Instead of a ribbon bow, make a beautiful rose to wire or glue to the present as a beautiful addition to your gift. Choose a ribbon that matches or compliments the one you use for the main wrap. Spray a little perfume on the rose for an added (and unexpected) treat.

▲ Tuck a pretty rose in the most unexpected places—to accent a pretty candle centerpiece or as an individual table favor.

ribbon roses

A pretty lapel pin rose is easy to make. Just glue a pin back onto the finished rose. Use this variety of rose for wedding corsages and keep it forever. ▶

◀ Created to resemble a real rose on a stem, this beauty stands tall in a clear glass vase. The leaf was added by twisting a piece of green ribbon on with the floral tape stem.

Make an elegant wreath of roses ▶ by gluing the finished roses to a purchased wreath form using hot glue or a strong glue adhesive. Add a pretty bow a the top.

9-patch quilt block

Pretty soon you will be making all kinds of wonderful quilted pieces for everyone you know—after you learn just one basic block.

make it

14

What you need

- Small pieces of fabric in desired colors
- Ruler
- Scissors
- Needle
- Thread in colors to match the fabrics
- Straight pins
- Iron

There are some cool quilting tools you might want to buy—now that you can quilt!

special tips for this project

* Much of the magic of making beautiful quilt blocks and lovely quilted pieces is not only in the workmanship but in the choice of fabrics and colors. You can find wonderful fabrics and people to help you choose colors at local quilt shops and fabric stores.

* Choose the colors that you like to work with and use. Every part of quilting should be fun and working with your favorite hues makes it even better.

* Be accurate when you cut the pieces for making your quilt block. Ironing your fabric first makes it easier to get a nice clean edge when you cut. Use good quality scissors or a rotary cutter and mat. For information about these and other tools, see the Tool Box, page 154.

* Use paper and colored pencils to plan your design before you start. Just draw nine squares and color them in different patterns and arrangements to see which one you like best.

make it

Prepare your fabric pieces. Decide how big you want the finished quilt block or blocks to be. Cut the 9 small squares all the same size—making sure you add a seam allowance. For example, if you want your finished quilt block to be 9 inches square when you are all finished, make each small square $3\frac{1}{2}$ inches square. Quilters usually allow a $\frac{1}{4}$ inch seam allowance all the way around each block. After you have the squares cut, lay them out in the order you want them. Look at the diagrams on the next page for ideas. When you like the way you have the squares laid out, you are ready to sew your quilt block. You can use a sewing machine if you have one, or just hand sew them using the running stitch.

running stitch

1 **You will be sewing the squares together into strips.** Put the right sides together of the first two squares and pin with the straight pins if you need to. Sew the pieces together using a $\frac{1}{4}$-inch seam. You can use a sewing machine or the running stitch by hand. If you are sewing by hand, make the stitches small—not more than $\frac{1}{8}$ inch apart. Be sure to secure the thread at the end. Now add the other square to the first two squares. Make three sets of 3 squares each.

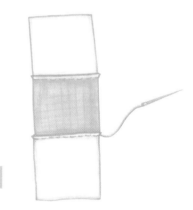

1

2 **Lay the three strips of squares side by side.** Match up the seams and with right sides together, pin them together. This will help to hold them in place. Sew the long sides together using the running stitch or a sewing machine. If you are sewing by hand, be sure and take small stitches.

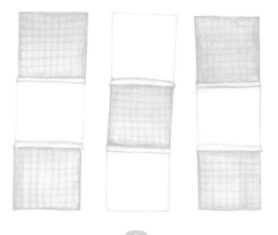

2

With an iron, press the seams to one side on the wrong side. Don't press the seams open. Press the seams in opposite directions to allow the seams to match up and lie flat. Turn the block over to the right side. You just made a quilt block!

3

take your designs to the next level

Look how easy it is to make your nine patch block unique by organizing the arrangement of your color squares in different ways. Below are just some of the color possibilities—of course there are hundreds you can create.

Combine bright batik-like fabrics with a soft neutral color to make pretty 9-patch blocks.

Use felted wool for an entirely different look. Instead of sewing the squares together with a running stitch, align the cut edges of the squares together and use an embroidery stitch to hold them together. Finish the edges with the buttonhole stitch.

Squares of color combine to make the coolest of quilt blocks.

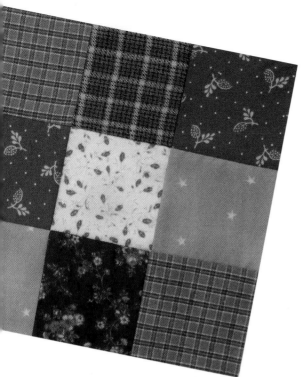

Try using all kinds of fabrics for your quilt block such as flannel, bright gingham prints, or polished cottons.

For a monochromatic look, choose colors all in the same color family, such as shades of blues or greens.

Make a signature block by having friends sign the squares in the finished block.

use it

▲ Make a pretty potholder with your finished block. Just cut a fabric backing from a plain piece of fabric the same size as the finished front block. Put double cotton batting between the two pieces and bind the edges using a 1-inch-wide strip folded in half or use purchased bias tape.

what else?

Make your pretty quilt blocks into all kinds of things. Use as the front of a pillow, make a tiny block and use on a greeting card, sew four together for a wall hanging, or sew many blocks together and make a quilt top or a tablecloth. You can hem, bind, or finish the edges any way you wish.

quilt block

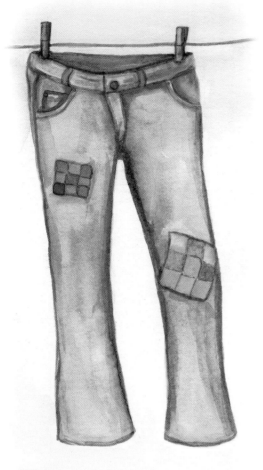

◄ Make small 9-patch blocks and use them for patches on a favorite pair of jeans. You can turn under the edges of the block when you sew it on the jeans or just stitch it on with the raw edge showing.

Use brown tones and tiny prints to make a simple untrimmed square table runner. Cut a piece of coordinating fabric the same size as the finished quilt block. Put a piece of quilt batting between the blocks and use the running stitch to make Xs as quilting stitches across the squares to hold it together. Leave the block edges unfinished. ►

scalloped paper boxes

Making a paper box seems almost like magic. You start with a simple sheet of paper and before you know it, you have created a 3-D work of art.

make it

What you need

- Tracing paper (unless you plan to photocopy the patterns)
- Sharp pencil
- Square of printed or plain-colored cardstock, or medium-weight paper at least 7x7 inches
- Ruler
- Scissors
- Rubber cement or other glue suitable for paper
- Clothespin

Try using two different colors of cardstock—one for the top and one for the bottom.

special tips for this project

❋ Cardstock paper works well for this project. Some cardstock comes in solid colors with a tone-on-tone texture. Printed medium-weight paper works nicely for this as well.

❋ You will need to score the lines on the box to make it fold right. Look for information about scoring paper in the Tool Box starting on page 154.

❋ You can vary the size of the box by enlarging or reducing the patterns that we have given you. Just photocopy it or scan it to the size you want.

make it

What you do

Trace the box top pattern, opposite, and the box bottom pattern, page 124, or photocopy them. Trace around the patterns onto the colored cardstock that you have chosen. Be sure to be very accurate when drawing around the pattern. It needs to be very accurate or it won't fit right. Mark all the lines on the pattern. Cut out the cardstock pieces.

1 **Open up the scissors or use a paring knife** to score the lines on the pattern. (See page 155 to learn about on scoring.) Scoring breaks down the fibers in the paper and allows for a clean fold. Score all of the lines on both the top and bottom pieces of the box.

2 **Fold on all of the scored lines** on the box top and bottom. The box will feel looser and you will see how it folds together. On the box bottom, the sides should fold in first.

3 **Apply the glue to both sides** of the corners in the folds of the bottom of the box.

4 **Bring the sides together** and use a clothespin to secure it while it dries. Glue all four bottom corners in the same way. After the glue dries, take off the clothespin.

5 **Glue the corners of the top of the box** using the glue to adhere the tabs to the lid sides. Let the glue dry. Put the top on the bottom of the box. You just made a charming little scalloped box! Fill it with something special!

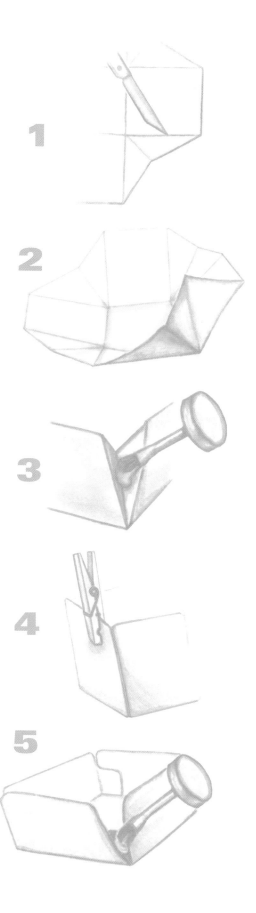

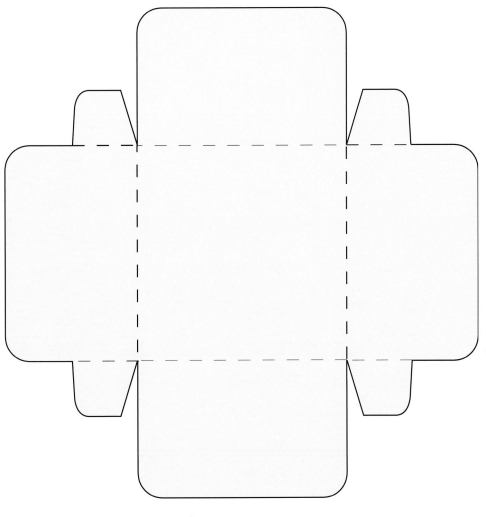

box top pattern

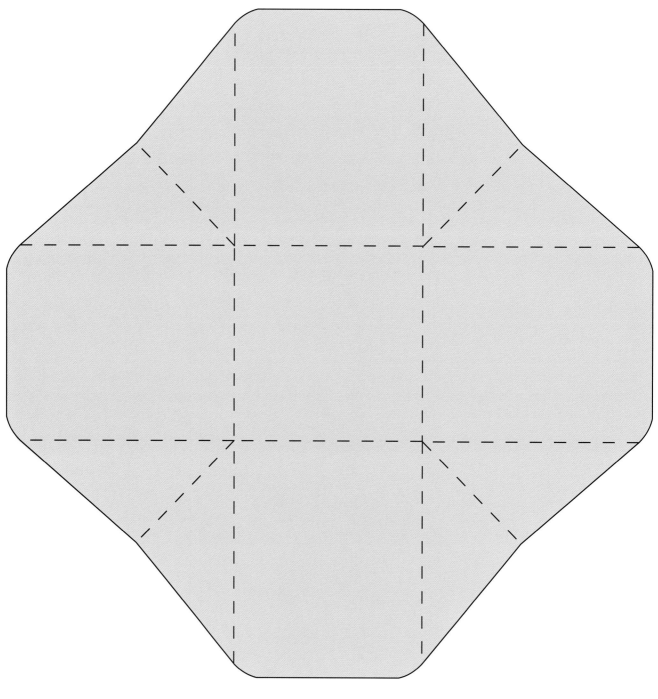

box bottom pattern

Precisely cut and folded, these boxes are a gift all by themselves.

Use a cardstock paper with a raised or embossed texture for the top of the box.

Add a design with a strip of graphic paper and repeat it by making a handle on top of the box. Just cut a strip of the paper and slide it between two slits on the box top. Add a drop of glue underneath to secure it.

Pretty pastels make this box perfect to hold a little girl's birthday wish.

Graphic shapes on the top of this box make it look beautifully contemporary.

125

Make the boxes out of pastel ▲
colors and use them to wrap little
baby gifts. All kinds of baby things
fit nicely in these handmade
boxes—little booties, pacifiers, tiny
socks, even a little T-shirt will fold
and tuck into the pretty box.

◀ Wrap the boxes with ribbon and then add something different to each one. Try candy canes, flowers, or a traditional bow to make each box special!

Fill the pretty paper boxes with candies, crackers, or lightweight cookies. These meringues tuck nicely in each handmade box. ▶

what else?

There are so many ways to make your box unique. Before you score and fold the box, try decorating it with rubber stamp designs. Or, after the box is all folded up and glued together, add some fun stickers on the sides and the top. Add a handle to the lid by gluing a loop of paper on the top.

easy knitted square

Love the look of knitting?
There are all kinds of things
you can make if you just
learn to knit a square (or
rectangular) shape. We'll
show you how to make a
simple and useful dishcloth—
then off you go! The
instructions for all
of the projects you
see in this
chapter start on
page 157.

Spicey Orange Scarf and
Sweet Blue Bag
instructions are on page 157.

make it

what you need

- For one dishcloth—(your practice piece) approximate size 11 x 9 ½ inches

- One skein of Lily Sugar n' Cream yellow cotton yarn (available at crafts and discount stores)

- Size # 8 knitting needles (available at crafts and discount stores); yarn needle

Don't be intimidated by knitting—it's just two needles and some yarn!

special tips for this project

❋ **Skeins of yarn:** If your yarn comes in a skein, then you will need to make the yarn into a ball before you start. The skein is just big loops of yarn that are gently twisted together. Just untwist it and starting with one end, make it into a ball so it won't get all tangled up when you are knitting. You can put it around a chair or let someone hold it for you with their arms stretched out like two goal posts. Whatever works is fine. You just need to get it into a ball.

❋ **Needles:** Knitting needles come labeled by number. The bigger the number, the bigger the needle. Using bigger needles is easier than using little ones. Your directions will tell you which ones to use.

❋ **Gauge:** Gauge is a way to check if you are knitting too loosely or too tightly. Every yarn has a gauge. This reflects the number of stitches it takes to knit an inch using certain needles. When you read the directions it will tell you the gauge and even remind you to "check your gauge". After you have knitted about 3 to 6 inches, lay out your work on a flat surface and check to see if your gauge matches what it should be. If you are knitting too loosely, your count will be under the gauge suggested. If you are knitting too tightly, it will be more than suggested. For the projects in this book, gauge is not that important. If your dishcloth or scarf is a little longer or shorter, it won't really matter. But if you are making something with pieces that fit together like a sweater, it would be very important. If you are just beginning to knit, it is just something you should know.

make it

what you do

If you haven't ever knitted before, it is a good idea to practice before you begin a project. We are going to show you how to make one of the Pretty Dishcloths shown on page 135 as a beginner project. That way your practice piece can really end up to be something you use! Instructions for all the projects in this chapter are on pages 157-159. In no time you will be making them all! Be sure to read the "Special Tips for this Project" on page 129 before you start. On page 157 you'll find the complete knitting instructions for making the Pretty Dishcloths. For right now we'll give you the instructions in separate parts. Don't worry. We'll show you how! These are the basic instructions: The gauge is 4 stitches per inch with size # 8 needles. You will cast on 45 stitches. Then you will knit every row for approximately 9¹/₂ inches. After that you will bind off and weave in the loose ends. That's it! Okay, Now it's time to learn how to knit and make your dishcloth.

Yarn

Making a Slip Knot and Casting On

First you will need to make a slip knot and cast on the stitches. That just means that you need to put a series of knotted loops—or stitches—on the needle to work with. The number of stitches that you put on will be the width of your piece. The length will be how long you make it.

There are many ways to cast on. It is really the trickiest part of knitting. It isn't hard but there is more than one way to do it. Some knitters cast on with two needles and some with one needle. The way we show you works well if you are right or left handed and if you have trouble holding the needles. Hold the needle however it feels comfortable—even vertical if that helps. However

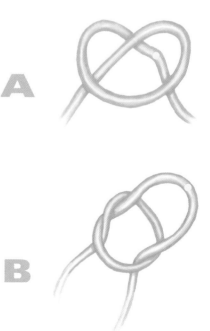

A

B

you cast on, first you need to make a slip knot. Pull the yarn out from the yarn ball to be about 2 yards long. Depending on how wide you want to make your knitted piece, the piece could be longer or shorter. But for practice, just pull out about 2 yards from the ball and make a slip knot there. The 2 yards that you pulled out will be what you use to cast on the needle. To make a slip knot:

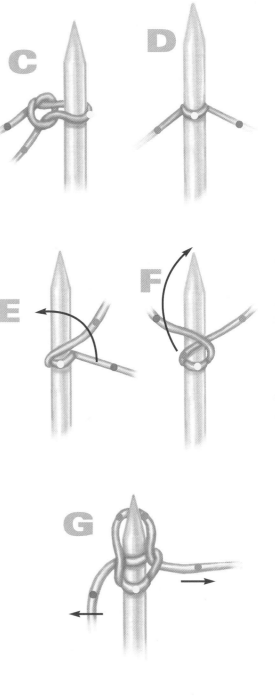

1A Make the yarn (leaving the 2 yard tail) into a pretzel shape.

1B Reach in and pull the yarn through the loop (we marked it with a yellow dot). You just made a slip knot!

1C Loop it over the end of your needle and pull it up to fit the needle. Keep the slip knot loose enough so that it slides easily along your needle. Now you are ready to cast on.

1D Swing the knot to the back. Keep the yarn that attaches to the ball (we marked with red) to the left. Keep the yarn that attaches to the loose piece to the right—we marked it with blue.

1E Take the red-dot yarn and bring it in front of the needle and up to the right. Bring the blue dot yarn over the red.

1F Reach under the blue dot yarn and grab the red dot yarn and pull it (making a loop) over the top of the needle.

1G Pull both the blue and red yarns. You just cast on one stitch. WOW! Continue to do that until you have as many stitches as you want or as many as the directions tell you to do. Our directions say, "Cast on 45 stitches". Keep the stitches that you cast on loose enough to slide on the needle. When you are first knitting, you will probably make them too tight. Remember that you will be putting the knitting needles in these stitches. To make the dishcloth, cast on 45 stitches.

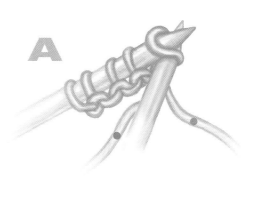

The Knit Stitch

Now you are ready to learn the knit stitch or the garter stitch—which is knitting the knit stitch in each row. This is a basic stitch for all knitting. This is the only stitch you need to make the projects in this book. Because you cast on with one needle, both ends of the yarn are at the top. The short yarn even got shorter because you used it to cast on. From now on you will use the yarn that comes from the ball of yarn. Now you are ready to start the knit stitch.

2A Move all the stitches that you cast on to the needle to the underside. This is the left needle. (In the illustration, we are only showing a few stitches. If you are making the dishcloth, you will have 45 stitches.) Move your work towards the end of the needle. Put the right needle up through the first loop, making sure it goes behind your left needle.

2B Using the yarn that comes from the ball (marked in red), loop it under and then back around the right needle end.

2C Catch that loop on the right needle and bring that loop through the first stitch on the left needle. You will be moving the right needle to the front of your work.

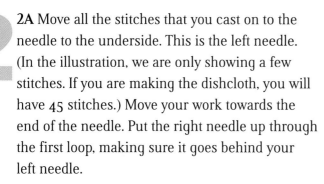

2D Continue pulling it, and slide it off of the needle. Be careful you only pull off one stitch and that the rest of the stitches stay on the left needle.

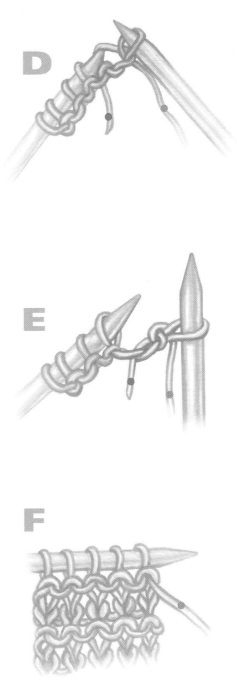

2E Now you have a stitch on your right needle. Put the right needle back into the next loop on the left needle just like you did in 2A and continue doing the knit stitch until you have removed all of the loops from the left to the right needle. Turn the right needle over, keeping your stitches at the bottom. This is now your left needle. Your right needle is the one with nothing on it. Now do it all again! Every time you do this you will be making a row of stitches.

2F When you are making a project, you will do this for as long as the directions tell you to do it. Your knitting stitches will look like this.

Practice until you feel comfortable with the knit stitch. All of the projects in this book are made using the knit stitch—also called the garter stitch. When you are really making a project, just do what it tells you until it is complete. Our directions for the Pretty Dishcloth tell you to knit until it is about 9 1/2 inches long. Then you are ready to bind off or cast off. This is really tying off the last row so it doesn't all come unraveled. Turn the page to see how to bind off.

Binding or Casting Off

Binding off is just a way of keeping your stitches from falling out and coming unraveled. It finishes your project with a nice edge.

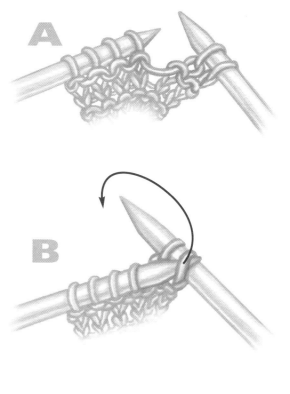

3A Knit the first two stitches as you did before for the knit stitch.

3B Now, use the left needle to pick up the first loop (the one farthest from the point) on the right needle.

3C Pull it up and over the second loop. The loop should drop off the left needle.

3D You just bound off your first stitch. There should be one loop on the right needle.

Now knit another stitch. Then lift the first loop on the right needle over the second just as you did in steps B and C. Continue doing this until there is just one loop left. It should be on the right needle.

You can cut the leftover yarn now, but be sure and leave a tail about 5 inches long. Pull that tail through the last stitch and pull it tight. You just learned how to bind off! Thread that little end of yarn into a yarn needle and weave it in and out of the finished piece to hide it. Wow! You just made a cool cotton dishcloth that you will love forever.

For more things you need to know about knitting, including how to add yarn if you run out, sewing seams, making fringe, blocking, and weaving in, see page 156. All the instructions for making the projects in this chapter start on page 157.

Knitting has never been so much fun—go ahead and cast on!

Knit a pretty and oh-so-fashionable scarf in no time with a novelty yarn that works up quickly. Instructions for the Aqua Scarf on on page 157.

Use the buttonhole stitch to finish the edges of a Clever Napkin Ring that you can knit in an evening. Instructions are on page 158.

You can knit with all kinds of fibers—this Bright Coin Purse was made using a variegated ribbon. Instructions are on page 157.

use it

what else?

There is really no limit to what you can knit now that you know how to make a knitted square. Rectangles and squares can turn into purses, eyeglass holders, neckties, extra long scarves, leg warmers, yoga mats, school bags, and even afghans.

▲ You'll love doing dishes with these Pretty Dishcloths that work up quickly using cotton yarn. The complete instructions for making these colorful kitchen accessories are on page 157.

knitted square

You'll feel cozy, pretty, and so proud of yourself, too, after you knit this Tweed-like Scarf with a fun fiber fringe. Make it in colors to match your favorite winter wear. Instructions for this project are on page 158.

A simple knitted square turns into a stunning and Colorful Place Mat that is perfect for most any color of dishes and flatware. The piece works up so quickly you can make enough to give as gifts! Complete instructions for making the place mat are on page 158.

sweet handmade soaps

You'll feel like a sculptor as you form these beautiful and smooth pieces of art. Slice them to see what glorious creations you have made!

make it

What you need

- Blocks of glycerine soap from a crafts store in the colors you like
- Blocks of coconut oil soap from a crafts store in colors you like
- Sharp knife
- Glass measuring cups
- Microwave
- No-stick cooking spray, such as Pam
- Bread pan or other mold (glass or metal)

Soap isn't for just cleaning anymore— it is an art form!

special tips for this project

❋ To make the soaps you will need to buy the soap blocks at crafts or discount stores. Sometimes using old soaps work, but most of the time these soaps do not melt well and have so many added ingredients that they do not blend together well. See the Tool Box on page 154 to learn more about buying blocks of soap.

❋ Choose the colors that you like. If you can only find clear soap blocks, purchase the soap coloring that is available in the same soap-making section of the store.

❋ Slicing the soap isn't hard, but be careful. If you have a band saw, it works great!

make it

What you do

First, decide what colors of soap you want to make. Choose a main color and colors for the little pieces that will be the design in the soap. You can mix the glycerine and coconut types of soap. The coconut melts just a little more quickly than the glycerine. You need to pick what color and type your main soap will be. Then decide what color you want for the pieces in the soap. You can't make a mistake—it will all turn out to look beautiful no matter what you choose! Spray the pan with the non-stick cooking spray and set the pan aside.

soap pieces

1 **Use a sharp knife** to cut long rectangular pieces from the colored soaps that you want for the pattern in the soap. Cut them right off the block into pieces about ¹/₂-inch wide and 2 or 3 inches long. They can all be different sizes. Don't worry, you can't make a mistake doing this. It will work no matter what size you use. Set them aside.

2 **Cut up the main color soap** that you have chosen into little pieces. Put them into the measuring cup. Put the cup into the microwave and melt on high for about 1 minute. They will melt very quickly. Watch carefully because it will bubble up if it melts too long.

3 **Take it out of the microwave.** Pour a thin layer into the bottom of the pan. It will set up almost immediately.

4 **Before it is completely set**, lay the cut pieces of soap on that layer in any arrangement you wish. You can overlap the pieces, lay them sideways or whatever you like. You are the artist! Don't wait to long, though, the next layer needs to be put on before the bottom layer gets too cold.

5 **Melt more of the main color soap** in the microwave and pour this main color over the soaps in the pan. Let the soap harden for at least 5 hours. Remove it from the pan. If it doesn't come out easily, put the soap in the refrigerator for a few minutes to cool.

6 **Using a large sharp knife,** carefully cut the soap into slices about 1- to 1 $\frac{1}{2}$-inch-wide slices. How exciting to see the beautiful soap you have made! Use it yourself or wrap in clear plastic wrap, add a colorful ribbon, and give as pretty gifts!

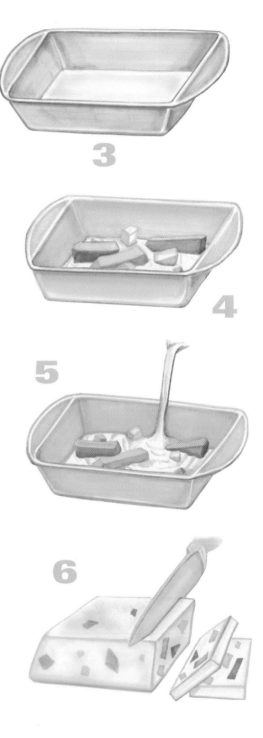

3

4

5

6

So beautifully subtle, this rounded bar of soap was designed with pieces of pastel glycerine shapes.

Combining glycerine and coconut soap (colored with just a touch of green) makes these soaps seem cool and clean.

These rectangular pieces of soap were made by slicing up soap that was poured into a small plastic square dish.

Many common containers make great soap molds. These shapes were sliced after the soap was made in a plastic disposable drinking glass.

Clean up your act by making some beautiful and clever soap shapes.

A bright pink background color silhouettes the white coconut soap shapes.

Poured into a bread pan before slicing, this soap has a stand-up shape.

use it

what else?

There are many ways to get color and shape into your soaps. Make a layer of colored soap and let it set. Use tiny cookie cutters or aspic cutters to cut shapes from that layer. Drop those shapes onto the first layer of soap and cover with the main color of soap. When you slice it, you'll see the pretty shapes you put in.

▲ Use bright, intensely-colored glycerine soap pieces surrounded with white coconut soap as the main color for a striking combination. Every slice will be a beautiful surprise.

◀ Make pretty soap cubes using just layers of different colors of soap. Cut them into tiny cubes to use as individual guest soaps.

▲ Instead of cutting long rectangles for the design in the soap, cut thin strips and coil them before laying them in a curve-topped pan. Pour the main color over as before. How contemporary!

Group different kinds of your ▲ soap creations together and set on a pastel towel in the guest room.

pop-up cards

It is always fun to make
handmade cards, but this card
has a special surprise inside!
Only you will know the secret of
making your greeting card pop
with what you want to say!

make it

What you need

- 7x7-inch square of light to medium weight paper (the square can be most any size but start with this size to learn how)
- Pencil
- Ruler
- Scissors (decorative scissors, optional)
- Adhesive such as a glue stick
- Trims such as stickers and colored papers

Just think of all the cool things you can put on the pop-up portion of your card!

special tips for this project

- Because the paper is folded to make the pop-up part of the card, the paper cannot be too heavy. Lightweight cardstock works well.

- Try all kinds of trims on your cards. Stickers, rubber stamps, and ribbons are just some of the things you can glue to your card. To learn more about some of the trims mentioned, see the Tool Box on page 154.

- If you plan to use an envelope with your card, find the envelope first and then design the card to fit the envelope. Making envelopes is kind of tricky and there are pretty ones in every color available at crafts and discount stores.

make it

What you do

Decide on the kind and color of paper you are going to use. Then decide on the size. If you have the envelope that you want to use, make the finished folded card about $1/4$-inch smaller than the envelope. Now that you have those decisions made, you are ready to make your card.

1 Fold the paper in half and then in half again. Use your finger to crease the edges so they are nice and flat.

2 Open up the paper so the fold is on the left side. Mark the corners with A and B as shown in the illustration. This will help you remember which way to fold the card so it will pop out. With a pencil, lightly mark where you will making the two slits on the left folded edge. Refer to the diagram on the next page to get an idea of about how far apart to cut the slits. These dimensions work well if you start with a 7x7-inch piece of paper. You can vary the dimensions quite a bit and the card will still work. Practice using some scratch paper first if you like. You can make the card square or rectangular shapes after you experiment a little and see what you like.

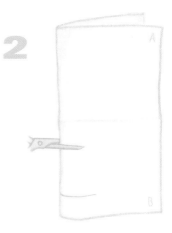

3 Open up the card and fold the A corner to the back to meet the B corner leaving the B corner in the right hand side. Recrease the top of the card.

4 **Fold the left side of the card over** as if folding the card, pushing the center crease inward and the pop=up outward. Open it back up. The pop-out part will pop out! You may have to gently pull the little box out to get it started—but then it will work all by itself.

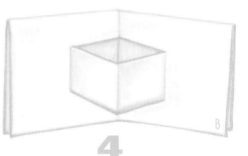

5 **Fold the card back and forth a few times,** to make the pop-up part adjust to popping out every time. Close the card and decorate the front. Decorate the pop-up part as well. The card can be used as shown in the illustration or you can make it open from the top. Now you'll be making these cute little cards for everyone you know!

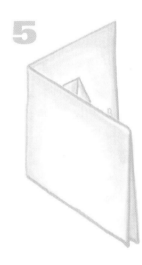

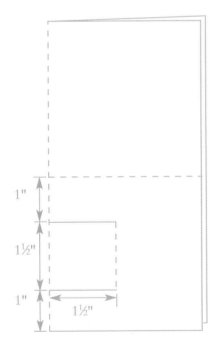

pop-up card
cutting diagram

1"

1½"

1"

1½"

Pretty and lacey stickers combine with a cut piece of doilie for an elegant look.

Send a pink and girlie greeting by adding some fun-foam stickers to your pop-up card.

congratulations

Add a little tiny element of surprise to a special baby card.

With just a little paper you will have some pop-up fun!

Use origami paper to make a sweet little greeting or for a wedding shower invitation. Add a pretty umbrella to pop out as a little surprise.

you are invited

Tuck some money in the pop-up part of a bon voyage greeting.

Use 3-D button-type stickers to spell out what you want to say.

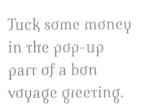

Have a Great Trip!

what else?

Because the pop-up cards can be made any size you choose, there are so many ways to use them. Make tiny cards using the paper from old Christmas cards to use on presents. Tuck a birthday greeting card in a present as a bonus surprise. Line up cards on a mantle with a different letter on each one to spell out a message.

▲ Make a gift card by cutting the edges with pinking shears and then adding a 3-D sticker to the pop-up center section. Write the name with a gold paint pen.

◀ Make a simple but extra-special greeting by adding two little hearts cut from red and purple cardstock to the pop up portion of your pretty little card. Add a heart in each corner to complete the lovely card.

Use vellum to make a ▶ stunning card to use as a namecard on any pretty tabletop. Add the initial of the guest to the pop-up section. Add dots of glue and dust with a little glitter to complete the placecard.

153

Acrylic Paint Any paint that has a plastic chemical base (not oil-based), is usually water soluble, and comes in small jars or bottles. Available at crafts, discount, and art stores.

Balsa Wood Lightweight wood available in stick or flat pieces used for crafting. Available at crafts, discount, and hardware stores.

Beading Wire There are dozens of kinds of beading wire available at crafts, discount, and beading stores. The wire is thin and strong and works well with crimping tools and beads. Usually comes on a roll.

Candle Scent Packaged in little bottles and usually placed by the candle wax, this product is made to add scent to candles. Available at crafts stores.

Candle Wax This wax usually comes in clear big blocks, but can also come in pieces in bags. Available at crafts stores.

Candle Wicking Sometimes woven, sometimes braided, and sometimes with a wire in the middle, this string-like material comes in small amounts in packages (usually displayed by the candle wax or on big spools for the serious candle maker). Available at crafts stores.

Cardstock This medium to heavy weight paper comes in all colors—available at crafts, discount, and scrapbooking stores.

Chenille Stem Often called a pipe cleaner, these long fuzzy stems can be found at crafts and discount stores and cost pennies each.

Craft Glue and Adhesive There are dozens of types of glue on the market for every special crafting need. White glues, clear glues, glue sticks, paper glues, fabric glues, and extra strong glues such as E6000 can be found at crafts, discount, and fabric stores.

Craft Wire Wire for crafting comes in every possible color and size. The size is usually measured by gauge with the higher the number of the gauge, the smaller the wire. It can be found at crafts, discount, and hardware stores.

Coconut Soap This opaque soap is made from coconut oil and is available usually in white only at crafts stores.

Crimp Beads Tiny flat metal beads designed to be squeezed shut at the end of a beading wire to hold the beads on the string. Cost varies on whether they are sterling silver or less expensive metal. Available at bead and crafts stores.

Decorative-edge Scissors Often made of colored plastic, these inexpensive scissors are made to cut pretty edgings on paper or other easy-to-cut materials. Available at crafts, discount, scrapbook, and fabric stores in a variety of styles.

Dowel Long, thin, round or square pieces of wood used for crafting and woodworking. Available at crafts and hardware stores.

Elastic Bead Cording Thin, often stretchable cording designed to use for beading. This inexpensive cording is available in many thicknesses at crafts stores.

Embroidery Floss This common and inexpensive product comes in hundreds of colors and usually comes in 6-strand lengths. Designed for embroidery, this fiber is great for a number of other crafts as well. Available at discount, fabric, and crafts stores.

Felt This non-woven fabric comes in acrylic or wool and works well for many crafts. The acrylic felt is available at crafts, discount, and fabric stores and is very inexpensive. The wool variety is available in crafts and fabric stores and costs a bit more.

Felted Wool This popular technique is created by washing wool felt in hot water and drying it in the dryer to shrink it. It leaves the felt beautifully soft with a wrinkled texture.

Floral Tape This tape (usually green) is used by florist to wrap wires and stems. Also available at crafts and discount stores, this tape needs to be pulled to release the stickiness.

Fusible Bonding This thin and fabric-like material, when placed between two pieces of fabric, will seal or bond them together making them seem like one fabric. Available at crafts and fabric stores.

Gauge A knitting term that refers to measurement in knitting. See page 129 for a full descriptions as this applies to knitting.

Glass Paints Developed only for painting on glass, these paints come in a variety of brands. Some manufacturers require that the paints be baked before using. Some can be air-dried. Not all are safe for use with food. Available at crafts and some fabric stores.

Glycerine Soap This transparent soap comes in blocks to be used for soapmaking. Oftentimes available in a variety of colors, it can be found at crafts stores.

Perle Cotton Sometimes spelled pearl cotton, this common embroidery fiber comes in dozens of colors and is sold in fabric and crafts stores. Inexpensive and easy to use, one strand is adequate to embroider most stitches.

Pinking Shears These were the first decorative-edge scissors designed to cut fabric in zigzags. Available at crafts, discount, and fabric stores.

Plastic Fun Foam Available at crafts, and discount stores, this flat, colorful plastic foam comes in all colors and shapes to be used for various crafting projects.

Polymer Clay This plastic-base clay comes in all colors and from many companies, such as Sculpey and Fimo. It needs to be baked in a conventional oven to make it permanently durable. The little blocks vary in price depending on color and brand. Available at crafts stores.

Pony Bead A large plastic bead that is flat on both sides. Usually comes in packages in a variety of colors and is very inexpensive. Available at crafts, discount, and beading stores.

Quilting Thread Thread primarily used for quilting that is stronger and more durable than regular sewing thread. Available at farbric stores.

Rotary Cutter A quilting tool that resembles a small pizza cutter that is a must for cutting multiple squares with accuracy. Available at crafts and quilting stores.

Rubber Stamps Little blocks of wood with a rubber image designed to print using paint or ink. Available at crafts and discount stores.

Scrapbook Papers Medium to heavy weight papers that come in all colors and patterns—sometimes printed on both sides. Available at crafts, discount, and scrapbooking stores.

Scoring This technique is used in all paper folding projects to make crisp and clean folds. It is usually done by using an open pair of scissors or scoring tool with a ruler drawing the line with the sharp tool to break the fibers in the paper, thus making the fold sharp and clean.

Spray Adhesive A type of glue that is sprayed onto a surface usually to adhere two pieces of paper together. Available at art and crafts stores.

Stickers Available at crafts, discount, and stationery stores, stickers come in all kinds of designs and styles. You can find 3-D stickers, vellum stickers, and 2-D stickers for every possible theme.

Tacky Glue A thick white glue that can be used on paper, wood, and other craft materials. Available at crafts, discount, drugstores, and fabric stores.

Tapestry Needle A needle often used for embroidery with a semi-blunt end. Available at crafts and fabric stores.

Tissue Paper Very thin paper that comes in all colors usually used for wrapping gifts—available at crafts, discount, and drugstores.

Variegated Ribbon Ribbon that has more then one color on it. The colors usually slightly blend together. This ribbon is available wherever other ribbon is sold, such as at crafts, fabric, or discount stores.

Vellum A translucent parchment-type paper that comes in white or in colors. Available at crafts and scrapbooking stores.

Wire-edge Ribbon This easy-to-use ribbon comes with a fine wire on both sides of the ribbon strip making the ribbon easier to tie into bows and to keep its shape.

Yarn Needle A large (often plastic) needle with an eye or hole big enough for yarn to go through. Used for some embroideries and for weaving in yarn when finishing a knitting project.

Knitting Information and Instructions

for Projects shown on pages 128-137

Adding Yarn to a Project

Now that you know how to knit, you may wonder what to do if you run out of yarn in the middle of a project. If you read the directions carefully, it will tell you how much to buy but it may take more than one skein. If you need to add yarn, just use an overhand knot (like tying your shoe) and tie the end of the new ball of yarn to the end piece of yarn in your knitted project. Try to anticipate if you are going to run out so you can add it when you reach the end of the row. Weave in the new piece when you are done and trim the ends.

Sewing Seams

You can refer to how to work the running stitch and buttonhole stitch on pages 10 and 11. The projects on those pages use those stitches to sew up the sides of purses. When sewing knitted projects together, just use a yarn needle and the yarn suggested to work the stitches just as you would if using embroidery floss or other thread on other projects.

Blocking

Blocking is a way to make a knitted piece smoother and lie flatter. You don't have to block every project, but it makes it smoother and lay nicer. If you want to block the project, just lay the project between two towels and use a steam iron to steam the piece. Pin the piece to the towel and let it dry that way. It will be smoother.

Weaving In

This term refers to how to keep the final loose thread hidden and from hanging off when you finish a project. Just thread the yarn onto the yarn needle and weave it back and forth until you feel it is secure.

Making Fringe

Fringe is fun to make and is great to use on scarves. Decide if you want the fringe to be the same yarn as the main part of the project or a different color or style of yarn. If it is to be the same yarn, be sure you set aside enough to use. For a 4-inch-long fringe on a 6-inch long scarf you will need about 14 yards of yarn. You also need a crochet hook. Start by cutting the pieces of yarn twice as long as you want the finished fringe to be. For 4-inch fringe, cut 8-inch lengths.

A Fold the yarn in half. Poke the crochet hook through the first stitch on the end of the scarf. At the middle, loop the fringe piece around the hook.

B Gently pull it up through the stitch.

C Pull the loop under the two fringe pieces.

D Pull the loop up tight making a knot. Continue to add fringe all along both ends of the scarf spacing it out as evenly as you can. Wow—that fringe looks great!

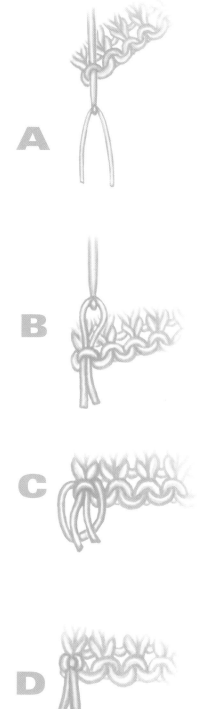

PRETTY DISHCLOTH(S)

(on page 136)
SKILL LEVEL: Beginner
SIZE: Approximately 9 $\frac{1}{2}$" x 11"
MATERIALS
Lily Sugar 'n Cream, worsted weight, 100% cotton yarn: One ball each of Yellow (00010), Rose Pink (00046), and Teal (01133)
Size 8 (5 mm) knitting needles or size needed to obtain gauge
GAUGE
In Garter Stitch (knit every row), 16 stitches = 4"/10 cm.
Take time to check your gauge.
INSTRUCTIONS
Cast on 45 stitches. Knit every row until piece measures approximately 9$\frac{1}{2}$" from beginning. Bind off. Weave in loose ends on one side of fabric. Make one dishcloth in each color.

SWEET BLUE BAG (shown, page 128)

SKILL LEVEL: Beginner
SIZE: Finished bag measures approximately 8" x 6$\frac{1}{2}$"
MATERIALS
Hilos La Espiga, No.18, 100% nylon cord: One spool Delft (22)
Size 3 (3.25 mm) knitting needles or size needed to obtain gauge
Yarn needle
1 yard of 1-inch-wide blue satin ribbon
Sewing needle and matching thread
GAUGE
In Garter Stitch (knit every row), 22

stitches = 4"/10 cm.
Take time to check your gauge.
INSTRUCTIONS
Cast on 44 stitches. Knit every row until piece measures approximately 16" from beginning. Bind off. Weave in loose ends on one side.
FINISHING
From cast on edge, fold up 6". Thread a 16" length of cord into yarn needle and sew each side in place. Turn right side out. Cut ribbon in half. Turn back $\frac{1}{4}$" at one end of each ribbon and finger press to form hem. Place a marker on center front of bag 2$\frac{1}{2}$" from fold; center hemmed end of one ribbon over marker and sew in place. Fold opposite edge of bag toward first ribbon, find center, sew remaining ribbon to top of flap near the edge. Tie ribbons into a bow.

SPICEY ORANGE SCARF

(shown on page 128)
SKILL LEVEL: Beginner
SIZE: Approximately 6$\frac{1}{2}$" x 56"
MATERIALS
Moda Dea, Aerie, from Coats & Clark, Art. R108, 100% nylon yarn (50 gram/1.76 ounce/71 yard ball): 3 balls Coral (9277)
Size 11 (8 mm) knitting needles or size needed to obtain gauge
GAUGE
In Garter Stitch, 12 stitches and 20 rows (or 10 ridges) = 4"/10 cm.
Take time to check your gauge.
NOTES: When adding a new ball of yarn, tie the ends and continue knitting. Weave in loose ends along

one side after all knitting is completed.
INSTRUCTIONS
Cast on 20 stitches. Knit every row for Garter Stitch until piece measures approximately 56" from beginning. Bind off loosely.

AQUA SCARF (shown on page 135)

SKILL LEVEL: Beginner
SIZE: Approximately 5" x 60"
MATERIALS
Moda Dea, Prima, from Coats & Clark, Art. R103, 60% nylon/40% polyester yarn (50 gram/1.76 ounce/82 yard ball): 3 balls of Turquoise (3527)
Size 10 (6.5 mm) knitting needles or size needed to obtain gauge
GAUGE
In Garter Stitch, 16 stitches and 26 rows (or 13 ridges) = 4"/10 cm.
Take time to check your gauge.
NOTES: When adding a new ball of yarn, tie the ends and continue knitting. Weave in loose ends along one side after all knitting is completed.
INSTRUCTIONS
Cast on 20 stitches. Knit every row for Garter Stitch until piece measures approximately 60" from beginning. Bind off loosely.

BRIGHT COIN PURSE

(as shown on page 135)
SKILL LEVEL: Beginner
SIZE: Approximately 4" x 5"
MATERIALS
Lion Brand Incredible, super-bulky weight, 100% nylon ribbon: One ball

of Carnival (205)

DMC Pearl Cotton, size #3: One skein in a bright pink hue

Size 4 (3.5 mm) knitting needles or size needed to obtain gauge

Size 6 (4 mm) knitting needles

Tapestry needle

GAUGE

With smaller needles in Garter Stitch (knit every row), 24 stitches=4"/10 cm.

Take time to check your gauge

INSTRUCTIONS

Beginning at the top with larger needles, cast on 24 stitches. Knit 6 rows. Change to smaller needles and knit 84 rows or until piece from beginning measures approximately 9". Change to larger needles and knit 6 rows for the second top. Bind off. Weave loose ends along one side of fabric.

FINISHING

Fold in half so tops meet. Thread two strands of Perle Cotton into tapestry needle. To Join Sides: Embroider buttonhole stitches from fold to last 6 rows at top; secure in place. (See Buttonhole Stitch diagram, page 11.) Repeat for second side.

Drawstring: Cut two strands of Perle Cotton, each 16" long. Thread both strands into tapestry needle. Beginning at center front of bag, weave in and out around bag and below the fourth ridge. Pull up so that the ends are even. Tie each end into an over-hand knot.

Tassel (make two): Cut two strands of ribbon measuring 6" each. Holding the strands together, tie around the Perle Cotton knot to form a tassel.

CLEVER NAPKIN RING

(shown on page 135)

SKILL LEVEL: Beginner

SIZE: Approximately 2 ^{3}/$_4$" wide x 5 ^{1}/$_4$" long

MATERIALS

Patons Grace, sport weight, 100% mercerized cotton yarn: One ball each of Ginger (225) and Viola (217)

Size 3 (3.25 mm) knitting needles or size needed to obtain gauge

Tapestry needle

GAUGE

In Garter Stitch (knit every row), 16 stitches = 2 ^{3}/$_4$"/ 7 cm.

Take time to check your gauge.

INSTRUCTIONS

With Ginger, cast on 16 stitches. Knit every row until piece measures approximately 5 ^{1}/$_4$" from beginning. Leaving a 10" tail at end, bind off. Thread tail into tapestry needle and sew ends together to form a ring. Weave ends along wrong side of ring. Turn right side out.

FINISHING

Thread a long strand of Viola into tapestry needle and work buttonhole stitch around one side of ring, securing in place at end. (See Buttonhole Stitch diagram, page 11.) Repeat for second side.

COLORFUL PLACE MAT

(shown on page 137)

SKILL LEVEL: Beginner

SIZE: Approximately 15" x 18"

MATERIALS

Plymouth Fantasy Naturale, worsted weight, 100% mercerized cotton: Two skeins Variegated (9951)

Size 8 (5 mm) knitting needles or size needed to obtain gauge

GAUGE

In Garter Stitch (knit every row), 17 stitches = 4"/10 cm.

Take time to check your gauge.

NOTE: When joining a new skein of yarn, tie ends together, then continue knitting.

INSTRUCTIONS

Cast on 63 stitches. Knit every row until piece measures approximately 18" from beginning. Bind off. Weave in all loose ends on one side of the place mat.

TWEED-LIKE SCARF WITH FRINGE

(shown on page 137)

SKILL LEVEL: Beginner

SIZE: Approximately 7 ^{1}/$_2$" x 38", excluding fringe

MATERIALS

Plymouth Encore Colorspun, worsted weight, 75% acrylic/25% wool yarn: Two balls Variegated (7125)

Lion Brand Fun Fur, bulky weight, 100% polyester yarn: One ball Tangerine (133)

Size 8 (5mm) knitting needles or size needed to obtain gauge

Size G/6 (4 mm) crochet hook

GAUGE

With Colorspun in Garter Stitch (knit every row), 17 stitches = 4"/10 cm.

Take time to check your gauge.

INSTRUCTIONS

With Colorspun, cast on 32 stitches. Knit every row until piece measures approximately 38" from beginning. Bind off. Weave loose ends along one side of the scarf.

Fringe: Cut one 12" length of Fun Fur. Fold in half to form a loop. Using the crochet hook, take the loop through first cast on stitch. Then take ends through the loop to form a knot. (See Fringe diagrams, page 156.) Make one fringe for each stitch along cast on and bind off edges.

Yarn Sources

Lily Cotton
100 Sonwil Drive
Buffalo, NY 14225
PHONE 1-800-265-2684
FAX 1-888-571-6229
www.sugarncream.com

The Plymouth Yarn Co., Inc.
500 Lafayette St.
Bristol, PA 19007
PHONE 1-215-788-0459
FAX 1-215-788-2269
www.plymouth.com

Lion Brand Yarn Co.
34 W 15th St
New York, NY 10011
PHONE 1-800-258-YARN (9276)
www.LionBrand.com

Patons
P.O. Box 40
Listowel, Ont.
N4W 3H3
PHONE 1-800-265-2865
www.patonsyarns.com

Hilos La Espiga
Located at your local Hobby Lobby

Coats
P.O. Box 1530
Albany, GA 31703
PHONE 1-800-445-1173
FAX 1-229-430-7427
www.modadea.com

ACKNOWLEDGEMENTS

Lyne Neymeyer (book design)

Lyne has designed dozens of books for various leading publishers across the country. She also teaches book design at the university level and brings a fresh and creative approach to every book she creates. A photographer as well as a designer, Lyne's talents are many as evidenced in the amazing and varied styles she is able to create in any and all of her design and photography work.

Kristen Krumhardt (illustrator)

With a degree in biological/premedical illustration, Kristen has a special talent of being able to draw what she sees with incredible accuracy. Also an avid crafter and talented artist, Kristen brings a fresh and beautiful approach to her precise drawings making them a delight to look at.

Dean Tanner (photographer)

A talented food and crafts photographer, Dean Tanner of Primary Image is best know for his great eye for composition and color in his work. His work can be seen in various books and magazines across the country including Better Homes and Gardens® Crafts magazines and Cuisine® magazine.

Pete Krumhardt (photographer)

Known across the country and the world for his beautiful photography, Pete is best known for his understanding of light and his work with gardens and nature. His work can be seen in numerous publications including Better Homes and Gardens® books and magazines.

Andy Lyons (photographer)

Best known for his creative approach for photographing people, Andy is also known for the liveliness he brings to all of his work in the crafts, food, and decorating areas. His outstanding work can be seen in book and magazine publications as well as advertising pieces across the country.

ABOUT THE AUTHOR

Carol Field Dahlstrom has produced over 75 crafts, food, decorating, children's, and holiday books for Better Homes and Gardens®, Bookspan®, and from her own publishing company, Brave Ink Press. She has made numerous television, radio, and speaking appearances sharing her books and encouraging simple and productive ways to spend family time together. Her creative vision and experience make her books fun as well as informative. She lives with her family in the country near Des Moines, Iowa, where she writes and designs from her studio.

Also from Brave Ink Press

If you liked this book, look for other books from Brave Ink Press:
- Simply Christmas
- Christmas—Make it Sparkle
- Beautiful Christmas
- An Ornament a Day
- College Kids Cook
- Creative Bone Series

To order books visit us at www.braveink.com

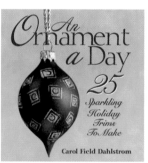

Brave Ink Press—the "I can do that!" books